DIY GUIDE
Appliances

Installing & Maintaining Your Major Appliances

Steve Willson

Creative Publishing
international

Creative Publishing international

Copyright © 2008
Creative Publishing international, Inc.
18705 Lake Drive East
Chanhassen, Minnesota 55317
1-800-328-3895
www.creativepub.com

Printed in China

10 9 8 7 6 5 4 3 2 1

Library of Congress Cataloging-in-Publication Data

Willson, Steven.
  DIY guide to appliances : installing & maintaining your major
appliances / Steve Willson.
      p. cm.
    Summary: "A comprehensive guide to instlling and performing basic
maintenance on all major appliances, including washers and dryers,
refrigerators, garbage disposers, dishwashers, water heaters, ovens
ranges and more"--Provided by publisher.
  Includes index.
  ISBN-13: 978-1-58923-330-0 (pbk.)
  ISBN-10: 1-58923-330-1 (pbk.)
  1. Household appliances, Electric--Maintenance and repair. I. Title.
II. Title: Do it yourself guide to appliances, installing and
maintaining your major appliances.

  TK7018.W55 2008
  643'.6--dc22

2007037930

President/CEO: Ken Fund
VP for Sales & Marketing: Peter Ackroyd

Home Improvement Group

Publisher: Bryan Trandem
Managing Editor: Tracy Stanley
Senior Editor: Mark Johanson
Editor: Jennifer Gehlhar

Creative Director: Michele Lanci-Altomare
Senior Design Manager: Brad Springer
Design Managers: Jon Simpson, Mary Rohl

Lead Photographer: Steve Galvin
Photo Coordinator: Joanne Wawra
Shop Manager: Bryan McLain

Production Managers: Laura Hokkanen, Linda Halls

Author: Steve Willson

Page Layout Artist: Kari Johnston
Photographers: Joel Schnell, Andrea Rugg
Shop Help: Dan Anderson, Cesar Fernandez Rodriguez,
Tami Helmer, John Webb

NOTICE TO READERS

For safety, use caution, care, and good judgment when following the procedures described in this book. The Publisher cannot assume responsibility for any damage to property or injury to persons as a result of misuse of the information provided.

The techniques shown in this book are general techniques for various applications. In some instances, additional techniques not shown in this book may be required. Always follow manufacturers' instructions included with products, since deviating from the directions may void warranties. The projects in this book vary widely as to skill levels required: some may not be appropriate for all do-it-yourselfers, and some may require professional help.

Consult your local Building Department for information on building permits, codes and other laws as they apply to your project.

CONTENTS

Introduction

appliances for many reasons: something may actually go wrong with the mechanical innards of a machine; or, the appliance may not have been operated following the manufacturer's instructions; or, the machine may not be receiving the correct amount of power or water. And sometimes an appliance may develop a problem simply because it was denied the regular maintenance attention that it needs to work efficiently.

In the DIY Guide to Appliances we show you how to install and maintain your major appliances properly, as well as how to repair them when things do go wrong. Appliance repair can be a very tricky and even dangerous task, so we have selected the projects shown based on what a novice home repairer might reasonably be able to accomplish.

NOTE: Major appliances and some smaller appliances come with a written warranty. Often, in order to activate the warranty, you are required to fill out and send in a card to the manufacturer. For most small appliances, the warranty is good for thirty to ninety days. To enforce the warranty, manufacturers will require that only an authorized repair person work on the appliance. If you work on the appliance yourself, be aware that the warranty may be voided.

Tools & Materials

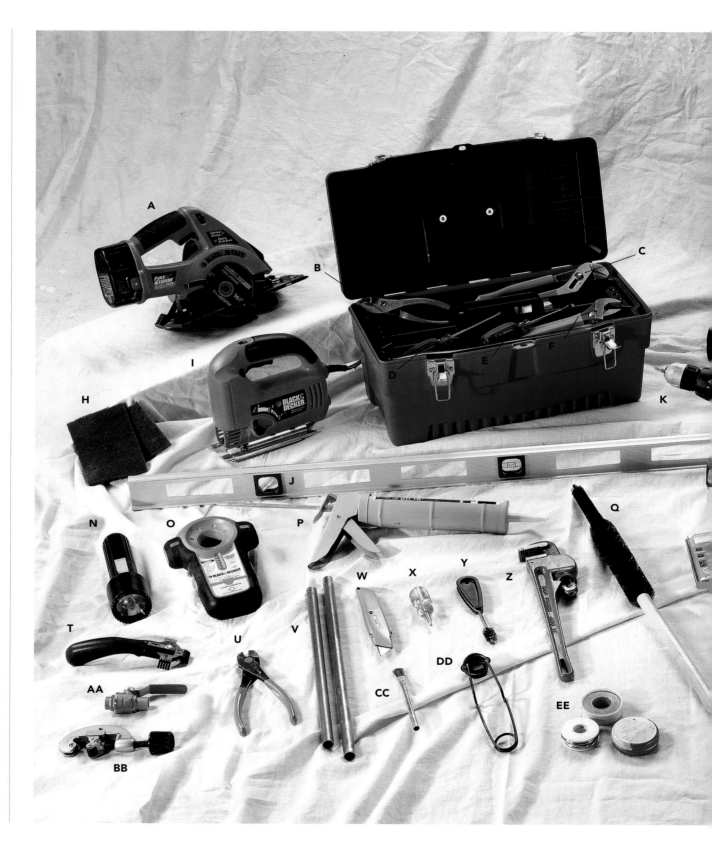

appliances doesn't require a boxful of specialty tools. A couple of screwdrivers and a wrench will take care of much of the work. But once you get into the area of making minor repairs, you'll begin to encounter some specialty tools. And, as the complexity of the repairs increases you'll find that the specialty tool requirements increase as well.

Many appliance repairs can be accomplished with basic hand tools you very likely own already. But as your tasks increase in complexity, you'll find occasional needs for specialty tools. Featured here is a fairly complete array of tools for the home appliance repair enthusiast.

(A) Cordless trim saw, (B) Pliers,
(C) Channel-type pliers, (D) Philips screwdriver, (E) Flathead screwdriver, (F) Adjustable wrench,
(G) Shop vac, (H) Abrasive pads,
(I) Jig saw, (J) Level, (K) Drill/driver,
(L) Measuring tape, (M) Propane torch,
(N) Flashlight, (O) Studfinder/laser level,
(P) All-purpose caulk/caulk gun,
(Q) Condenser coil brush, (R) Multimeter,
(S) Reciprocating saw, (T) Fin comb,
(U) Side cutters, (V) Copper pipe,
(W) Utility knife, (X) Small Philips screwdriver,
(Y) Cleaning brush, (Z) Pipe wrench,
(AA) Shutoff valve, (BB) Tubing cutter,
(CC) Flux brush, (DD) Igniter,
(EE) Soldering paste/Teflon tape,
(FF) Copper fittings, (GG) Steel brush,
(HH) Brass brush, (II) Hammer,
(JJ) Gloves, (KK) Needlenose pliers

Appliance Diagrams

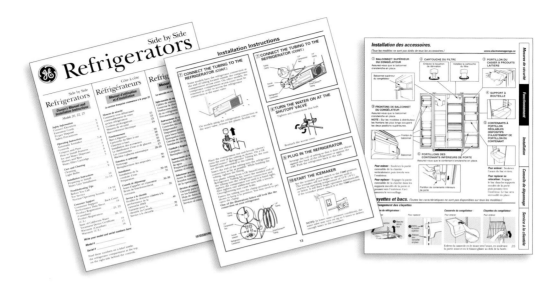

The owners' manual is an indispensable tool for making complex appliance repairs, especially if the repair requires that you order parts. These days, you can track down a manual for virtually any appliance using the Internet. All you need is the name of the manufacturer and the model number.

FOR MAKING APPLIANCE REPAIRS OF ANY REAL COMPLEXITY YOU NEED A DETAILED WORKING diagram. Most owners' manuals include such schematic roadmaps, along with parts lists and stock numbers that are absolutely critical, even for professionals. If you no longer have possession of the manual that came with your major appliance, go Online and search for a replacement. In some cases you may be charged a fee, but most major manufacturers maintain up-to-date archives of the manuals for their products. If you do not have Internet access you can also contact the manufacturer by telephone and most are happy to mail you a new manual.

Along with its value as a source for replacement owners manuals, the Internet has also become a very useful tool for locating and ordering replacement parts. There are several sites you may log onto that guide you through the process of identifying and addressing specific problems and then offer the opportunity to buy the exact part or parts that will (hopefully) solve your problem.

On the following pages you will find exploded-view illustrations of major home appliances. These working diagrams are intended to provide general information about the machines that populate each appliance category, but they are not sufficiently detailed to serve as technical guides for your specific appliance. You may use them to gain some familiarity with how the major parts and systems function, and this in turn may be of help as a troubleshooting reference and as a supplement to undertaking any of the installation or repair projects shown in detail in this book.

WASHING MACHINE

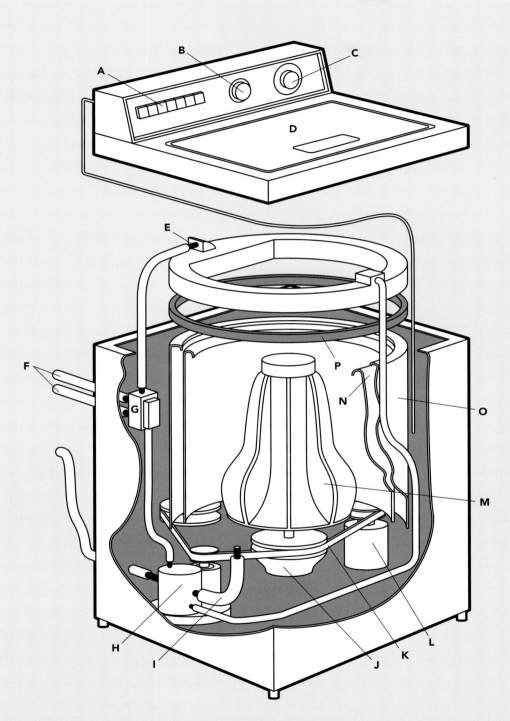

Washing machine parts include: (A) Selection switches, (B) Water level control, (C) Timer control, (D) Lid, (E) Inlet nozzle, (F) Inlet hoses, (G) Water mixing valve, (H) Water pump, (I) Water hose, (J) Transmission, (K) Transmission belt, (L) Motor, (M) Agitator, (N) Wash basket, (O) Tub, (P) Gasket.

CLOTHES DRYER

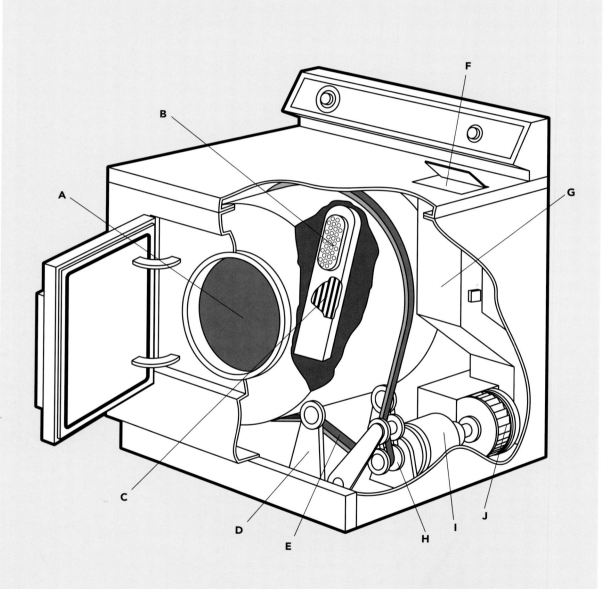

Clothes dryer parts include: (A) Drum, (B) Heating duct, (C) Heating element, (D) Drum support, (E) Drive belt, (F) Lint trap, (G) Exhaust duct, (H) Belt tension spring, (I) Motor, (J) Fan.

DISHWASHER

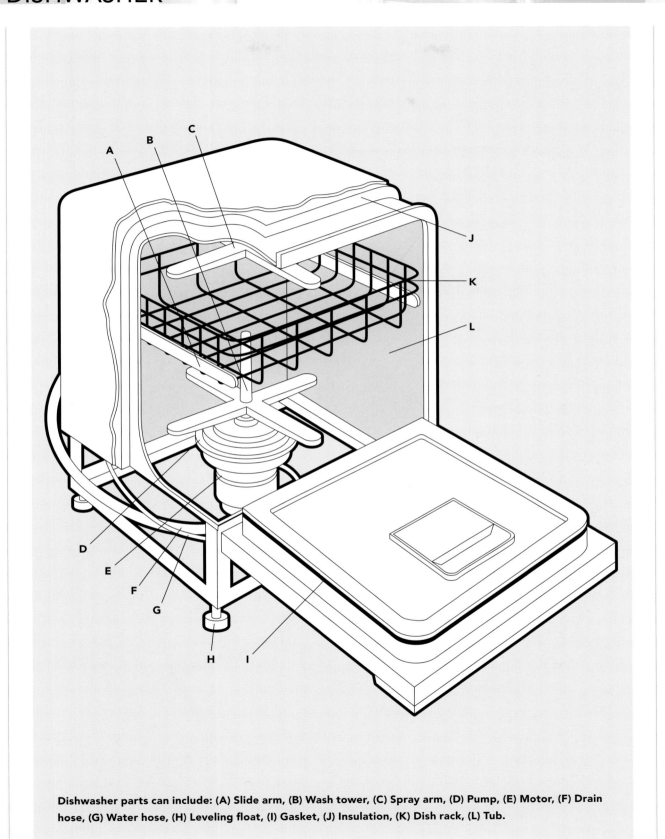

Dishwasher parts can include: (A) Slide arm, (B) Wash tower, (C) Spray arm, (D) Pump, (E) Motor, (F) Drain hose, (G) Water hose, (H) Leveling float, (I) Gasket, (J) Insulation, (K) Dish rack, (L) Tub.

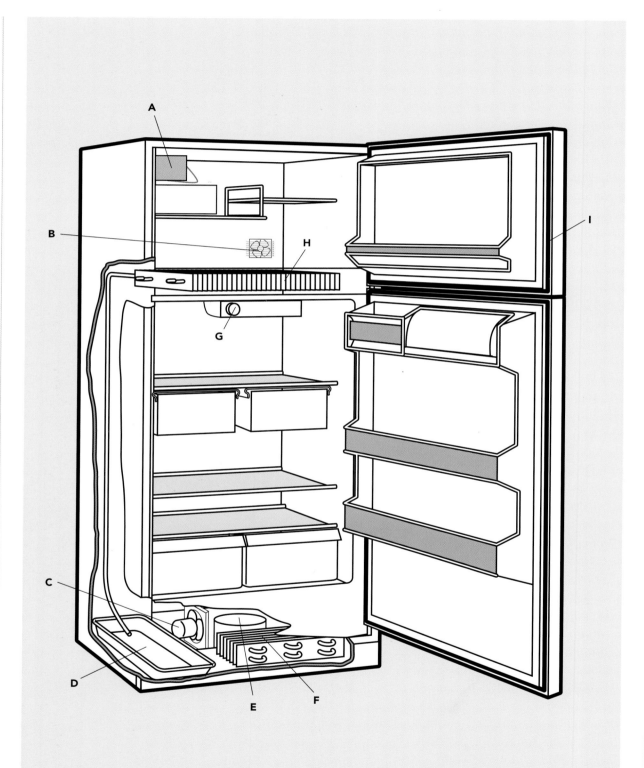

Refrigerator parts can include: (A) Ice maker, **(B)** Evaporator fan, **(C)** Condenser fan, **(D)** Drain pan, **(E)** Compressor, **(F)** Condesor coils, **(G)** Thermostat controls, **(H)** Evaporator coils, **(I)** Door gasket.

ELECTRIC RANGE

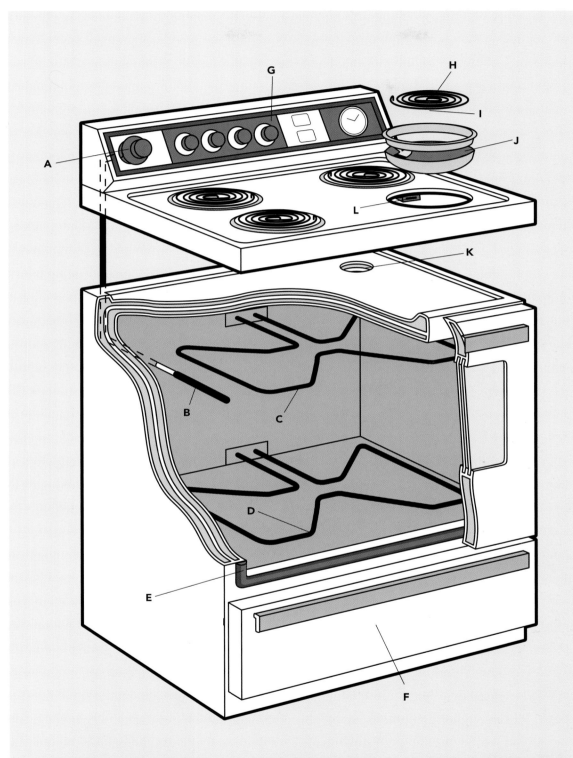

Electric range parts can include: (A) Oven thermostat, (B) Temperature sensor, (C) Broil element, (D) Bake element, (E) Gasket, (F) Storage drawer, (G) Control panel, (H) Heating element, (I) Element receptacle, (J) Element well, (K) Oven vent, (L) Element receptacle source.

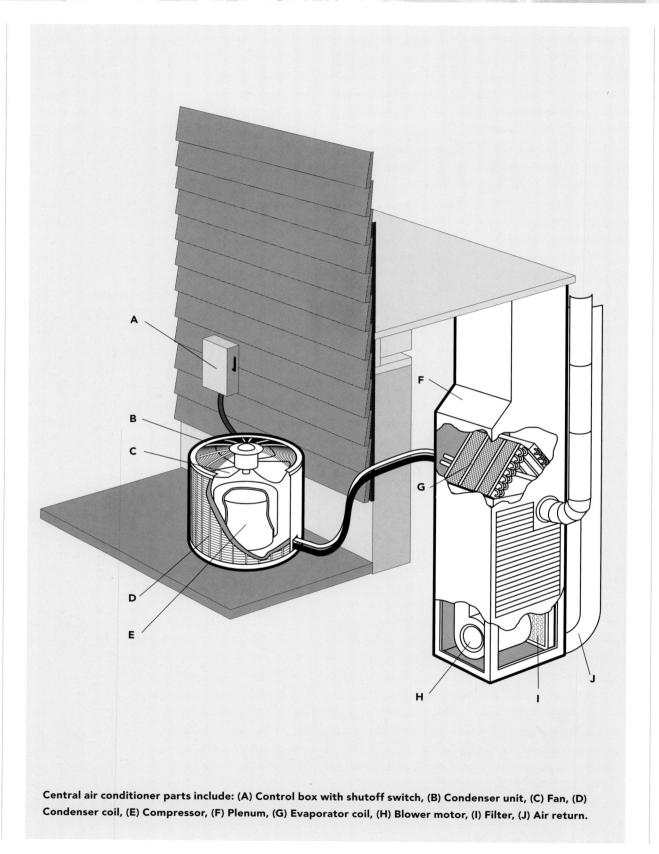

Central air conditioner parts include: (A) Control box with shutoff switch, (B) Condenser unit, (C) Fan, (D) Condenser coil, (E) Compressor, (F) Plenum, (G) Evaporator coil, (H) Blower motor, (I) Filter, (J) Air return.

GAS FURNACE

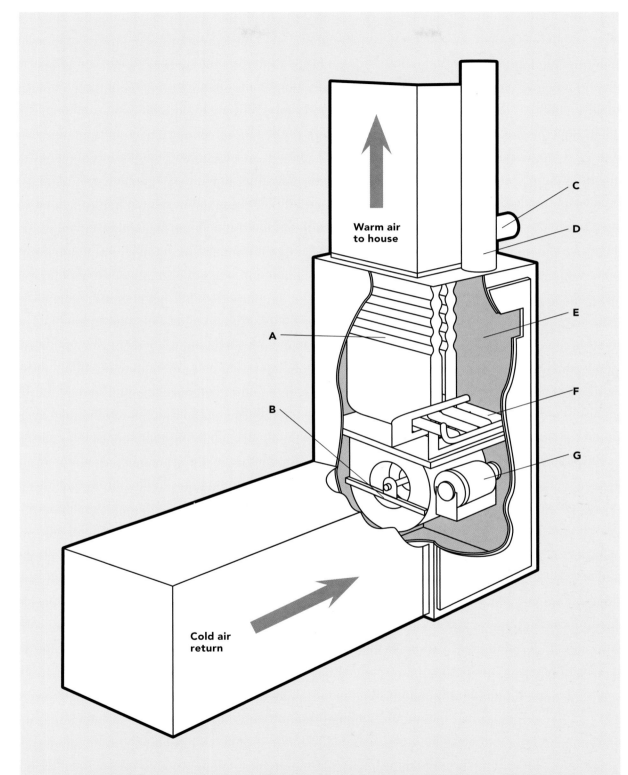

Warm air
to house

C

D

A

E

B

F

G

Cold air
return

High-efficiency gas furnace parts include: (A) Heat exchanger, (B) Circulating fan/blower motor, (C) Vent damper, (D) Vent connector/flue, (E) Combustion chamber, (F) Burners, (G) Blower motor.

GAS WATER HEATER

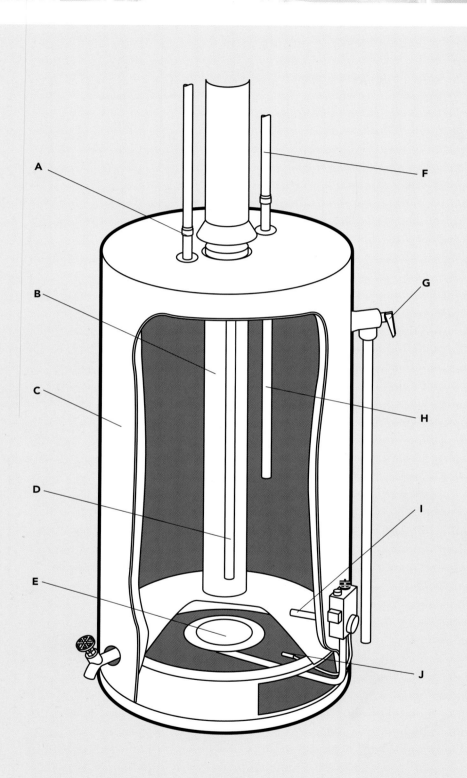

Gas water heater parts include: (A) Hot water outlet, (B) Flue, (C) Tank, (D) Anode rod, (E) Gas burner, (F) Cold water inlet pipe, (G) Pressure-relief valve, (H) Dip tube, (I) Thermostat (J) Thermocouple.

ELECTRIC WATER HEATER

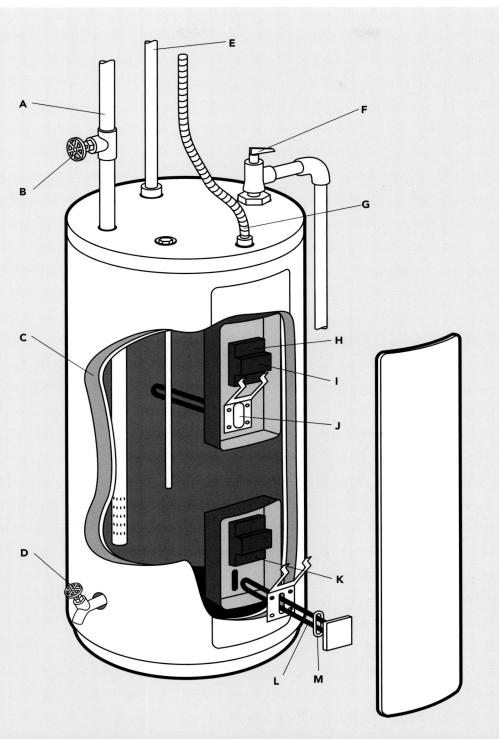

Electric water heater parts can include: (A) Cold water inlet pipe, (B) Cold water inlet valve, (C) Insulation, (D) Draincock, (E) Hot water outlet pipe, (F) Pressure relief valve, (G) Power cable, (H) High temperature thermostat, (I) Upper heating thermostat, (J) Bracket, (K) Lower heating thermostat, (L) Lower heating element, (M) Gasket.

Installation Projects

INSTALLING APPLIANCES YOURSELF HAS SEVERAL ADVANTAGES over hiring someone to do it for you. First, it saves you money ($50 or more in many cases). But it is also more convenient, especially if you choose to transport the appliance yourself. By handling both the transport and the installation, you can get the appliance into your home and have it working as soon as you buy it. No waiting for days to have it delivered and installed.

In this chapter we'll show you how to install eleven common home appliances, from major appliances like a dishwasher to smaller projects, such as a new thermostat. For a number of reasons, we do not cover installation of refrigerators and stoves in this book, although we do show how to hook up an icemaker and we give maintenance information later. Both of these appliances are unwieldy and dangerous to transport, so most appliance sellers offer reasonable delivery choices that typically include removal of the old appliance. If your stove or range is fueled with gas, we recommend (and many municipalities insist) that you hire a professional for the hookup.

THIS CHAPTER INCLUDES:

- ❏ Washing Machine
- ❏ Dryer Vent
- ❏ Dishwasher
- ❏ Water Heater
- ❏ Water Softener
- ❏ Range Hood
- ❏ Hot Water Dispenser
- ❏ Icemaker
- ❏ Reverse Osmosis Water Filter
- ❏ Room Air Conditioner
- ❏ Thermostat

Washing Machine

A WASHING MACHINE REQUIRES POWER, WATER, AND A CONNECTION TO THE DRAIN SYSTEM. These are all easy to provide if the hookups already exist. But if they don't, you'll need to make some choices about how much improvement and work you're willing to take on. If your room is not set up for a washing machine installation and you have a bit of experience in plumbing, you may want to install a washing machine standpipe drain as part of your project. These devices combine the drain and supply demands of a washing machine into a neat package that is less likely to create problems than a system where the drain hose from the washer is simply hooked over the edge of a laundry tub. In this project we'll show you exactly how to install a washing machine standpipe drain.

If your installation area is equipped with a 120-volt electrical circuit already, you should be good to go. If not, contact a qualified electrician to install a new circuit for you. Check to make sure the receptacle has ground-fault circuit interruption protection (GFCI), however. If it does not, either swap out the receptacle or have an electrician do it for you.

INSTALL A WASHING MACHINE

TOP-LOAD OR FRONT-LOAD?

There are two general types of washing machine: the top-loader (left) and the front-loader (right). If the machine is a top-loading type, an agitator in the tub goes back and forth or up and down to wash the clothing. In front-loading types, the drum is filled with water and soap and it spins to tumble the clothing clean. Front-loading types tend to be gentler on clothes than machines with agitators, but are considerably more expensive.

SAVING MONEY ON LAUNDRY DAY

About 80% to 85% of the energy used for washing clothes is for heating the water. You can reduce the amount of energy used for washing clothes by either using less water or by using cooler water. Unless you're dealing with oily stains, the warm or cold water setting machine will generally do a good job of cleaning your clothes. Switching your temperature setting from hot to warm can cut a load's energy use in half, and switching from warm to cold can reduce the energy consumption even more.

DIFFICULTY LEVEL

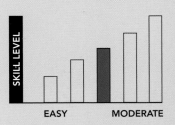

SKILL LEVEL

EASY   MODERATE

This project can be completed in a weekend.

HOW TO INSTALL A WASHING MACHINE

1 To move your new washing machine, consider renting an appliance hand cart from the local rental center. If necessary, cut away the protective cardboard box from the washer and remove the wood crating on the bottom of the unit.

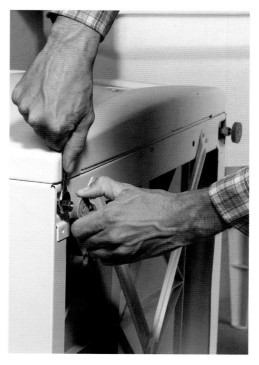

2 Loosen all four leveling leg locknuts so they will be easy to adjust later.

3 Attach the supply hoses that came with the washer to the shutoff valves or hose bibs. Place the open end of each hose in a bucket and briefly turn on the water to make sure the valves work properly.

4 Connect the other ends of the hoses to the in-let ports at the back of the washer. Tighten the fittings in a clockwise direction with channel-type pliers.

5 Slide the washer against the wall and check the top for level from side-to-side and front-to-back.

6 If leveling is necessary, tip up the machine and thread the adjustable legs in and out until the machine is stable and level.

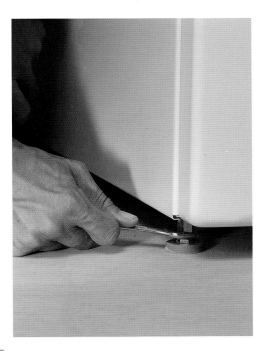

7 Once the legs are adjusted, tighten the lock-nut on each one so that machine vibrations won't loosen the legs. Install a plastic foot on the bottom of each leg.

WET BASEMENT?

If your washing machine (or any other appliance) is installed in a basement, you can protect it from the threat of minor flooding by installing it so it is raised off the floor. Make sure the platform is strong and stable. Concrete patio pavers are one good choice for raising the machine. Or, you can build a platform from scrap wood and plywood.

STANDPIPE DRAINS

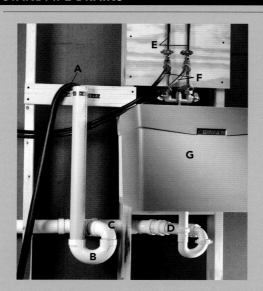

In many houses, the washing machine drain hose is hung loosely over the side of the utility sink, but this configuration is frowned upon by building codes. Instead, you should install a standpipe drain that allows the washing machine to drain directly into the utility sink's drain line. Standpipes with attached P-traps can be purchased at many home centers. A 2"-pipe is required by most building codes. The top of the standpipe should be higher than the highest water level in the washing machine, but not shorter than 34". Hose bibs are installed in the hot and cold supply lines at the utility sink to provide the water supply to the washing machine.

A washing machine with standpipe drain: washing machine drain hose (A), 2" standpipe drain with trap (B), waste line (C), utility sink drain pipe (D), hot and cold supply lines with hose bibs (E), rubber supply hoses to washing machine (F), and utility sink (G).

1 Measure and mark the size and location of a waste Y-fitting in the drain line. Remove the marked section, using a reciprocating saw. Make cuts as straight as possible.

2 Use a utility knife to remove rough burrs on the cut ends of the pipe. Dry-fit the waste Y-fitting into the drain line to make sure it fits properly, then attach the Y-fitting using primer and solvent glue.

3 Dry-fit a 90° elbow and a 2" standpipe with trap to the waste Y-fitting. Make sure the standpipe is taller than the highest water level in the washing machine (a minimum of 34"). Solvent-glue all the pipes in place.

4 Attach a 2 × 4 piece of wood behind the top of the standpipe for support, using 2½" deck screws. Fasten standpipe to the wood support, using a length of pipe strap and ½" screws. Insert the washing machine's rubber drain hose into the standpipe.

HOW TO MAKE WATER SUPPLY CONNECTIONS

Install hose bibs in the utility sink supply lines. Turn off water main and drain pipes. Cut into each supply pipe 6" to 12" from faucet. Solder threaded T-fittings into each supply line. Protect wood from torch flame with two layers of sheet metal. Wrap Teflon tape around threads of hose bibs, and screw them into T-fittings. Connect a rubber supply hose from each bib to the appropriate intake port on the washing machine.

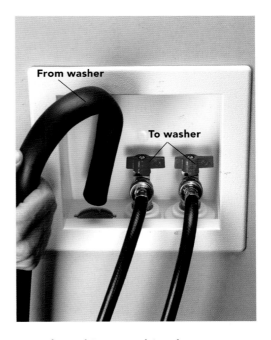

Recessed washing machine boxes are available for finished utility rooms. The supply pipes and standpipe drain run to one central location. The washing machine's hose bibs, supply hoses, and drain hose must remain easily accessible.

Dryer Vent

ELECTRIC CLOTHES DRYERS ARE SIMPLE TO INSTALL, BUT ONLY IF YOU ARE REPLACING AN OLD ONE with a new one of the same type. If your dryer is being installed in a new spot, you'll need to install a dryer vent. With the exception of expensive, ventless models that are not yet widely available, all dryers must be vented so the dryer exhaust is removed from the house efficiently. Each dryer model stipulates the length, diameter, and the proper material for the vent piping. The owners manual also stipulates how much length you have to deduct from an acceptable vent for each elbow you install in the line.

If you are installing an electric dryer in a spot that has never housed one before, or if you are replacing a gas dryer with an electric dryer, the project is much more involved. If you have some basic wiring and carpentry skills, you may be able to manage the project without too much difficulty. But if you are not comfortable with home electrical projects, contact a qualified professional for this part of the job. If you are running a new wiring circuit, you will need to obtain a permit from your local building department.

INSTALL A DRYER

PUT YOUR DRYER HIGHER

Because they do not require water supply and drain hookups, as washing machines do, dryers offer a bit more flexibility when it comes to installation area. You still need to make certain that the machine is vented properly, and that electrical or gas hookups are made safely. In the photo below, a stackable dryer is installed on top of a matching washing machine in much the same configuration as an all-in-one washer/dryer combination. This makes loading and unloading more comfortable.

TERMS YOU'LL NEED TO KNOW

VENT HOOD—A protective device that keeps water, snow, insects, and small animals from entering a dryer duct. It is made with a lightweight flapper that is opened outward by the exhausted air, then closes when the airflow stops.

TOOLS & MATERIALS YOU NEED

- ❏ Utility knife
- ❏ Hammer
- ❏ Screwdrivers
- ❏ Channel-type pliers
- ❏ Electric drill
- ❏ Hole saw
- ❏ Caulking gun
- ❏ 2-ft. level
- ❏ Silicone caulk
- ❏ Dryer vent hood
- ❏ Dryer vent duct and elbows
- ❏ Duct tape
- ❏ Perforated strapping

DIFFICULTY LEVEL

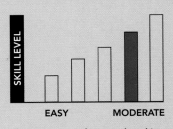

This project can be completed in a weekend.

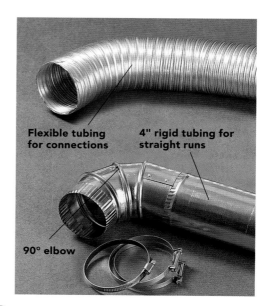

1 Confirm that the electrical receptacle you will be plugging your dryer into is appropriate for an electric clothes dryer. Most residential dryers require a 30-amp, 120/240 volt model.

2 Confirm that your current dryer vent is not made of flexible plastic tubing. This material is suitable only for low-heat exhaust, such as a bathroom fan vent, not for dryers. Dryers require 4" rigid metal vent pipe, except for connectors, which may be made of flexible metal tubing.

3 To plan your vent pipe route (they can be no longer than 25 ft. in most places), start outdoors by establishing the best location for the dryer vent hood. The ideal location is as close to the dryer as possible, but concealed from sight and kept away from windows. In most cases it is easiest to run the pipe through the rim joist of your house, but in some cases you may have to cut through a masonry foundation wall. Choose a spot and mark it with tape.

4 Look for a distinguishing point in the house structure that you can locate precisely on the interior side. A window, sillcock, or another penetration in the rim joist is perfect. Measure the distance from the point to the marked area where you want to install the vent hood.

5 On the interior side of the wall, generally in the basement, measure from the structural object you identified to see if the potential location for the rim joist entry is clear and accessible. Also check to see if you can make a relatively clean run to the dryer, with minimal turns and minimal cutting of floor joists. Finding the best spot will probably take some trial and error and compromising.

6 Outline a hole that's slightly larger in diameter than the vent fitting that will go through the wall. Drill through the hole center into the rim joist using a bit that's long enough to penetrate the exterior. Drill until the bit breaks through into the light of day. NOTE: Holes must be at least 2" from either edge of the joist and their diameter cannot be more than ⅓ of the joist width.

7 Using the drill hole in the siding as a center-point, draw the outline for the cutout on the siding of your house. Cut out with a reciprocating saw and remodeler's blade.

8 Remove the cutout section of siding and joist material and test the fit of the vent pipe assembly. Widen the hole if necessary.

(Continued)

9 Once the assembly fits, slide the vent hood and pipe assembly into the hole so the vent hood flange fits as snugly against the siding as possible. Attach the vent hood to the siding by driving screws at the corners.

10 Apply exterior-rated caulk around the perimeter of the vent hood to make a watertight seal. Snap on the protective cage, if provided, to keep small animals out.

11 Loosely pack fiberglass insulation between the vent duct and the edges of the opening you cut. Or, fill the gaps with minimal expanding spray foam insulation.

12 Run rigid metal ductwork from the vent hood to the dryer. If you can, plan the route so you're installing the ductwork in the floor joist cavity. This will leave more headroom and lessen the chance of damaging the material. Otherwise, suspend the ductwork from the bottom edges of the floor joists, supporting it with perforated strapping attached to the floor joists.

13 Install an elbow at the end of the horizontal duct so it connects to the vent hood. Then add a vertical duct to the other side of the elbow to bring the duct down to the dryer.

14 Attach a 90° elbow to the vent opening stub on the back of the dryer.

15 Push the vertical duct pipe into the top of the elbow fitting coming from the back of the dryer. Secure it with duct tape.

16 Plug in the dryer, push it against the wall, and check the top for level from front to back and side to side. Adjust the dryer feet as required to make the unit level.

Dishwasher

DISHWASHERS DO A LOT OF WORK AND HOLD UP PRETTY WELL. ACCORDING TO AHAM (Association of Home Appliance Manufacturers) the average useful life of a built-in dishwasher is thirteen years. That's the good news. The not-so-good news, but not-so-unexpected either, is that thirteen years is not forever. Eventually, your dishwasher will need to be replaced. The job isn't very difficult. If you have a pretty good assortment of tools and a well-stocked hardware store close by, you should be able to wrap it up in less than a day.

Fortunately, there's quite a bit of standardization in the dishwasher world. There are certainly performance differences between models, especially across the full width of the price range. But the way the machines are installed and the cabinet sizes are pretty universal. Just be sure to carefully review the installation directions that came with the appliance before you start any work.

INSTALL A DISHWASHER

EFFICIENT LOADING

In order to get the best possible circulation of wash water, which is called wash action, follow a plan when loading dishes into the dishwasher.

- Make sure they are loaded so water can reach all of the soiled surfaces.
- Be sure that larger items are not blocking smaller items from the wash action.
- Place all items in both racks so that they are separated and face the center of the dishwasher. This will help to ensure that water reaches all soiled surfaces.
- Place glasses with the open end facing downward to allow proper washing action.
- Do not place glasses over the tines, but between them. This will allow the glasses to lean toward the spray arm and will improve washing. It also promotes drying by reducing the amount of water remaining on the top of the glass after the wash cycle is complete.
- Do not allow flatware to "nest." This prevents proper water distribution between the surfaces.
- Load flatware, except knives, with some handles up and some down to prevent nesting. For safety, knives should always be loaded handles up.

TERM YOU'LL NEED TO KNOW

DISCHARGE HOSE LOOP—A loop installed in a dishwasher discharge hose, usually attached to the underside of the countertop, to keep waste water in the disposer from back-flowing into the dishwasher. The loop requires the water to do the impossible, namely flow uphill, to reach the dishwasher.

TOOLS & MATERIALS YOU NEED

- ❏ Screwdrivers
- ❏ Adjustable wrench
- ❏ 2-ft. level
- ❏ ⅝-in. automotive heater hose
- ❏ Teflon tape
- ❏ Cable connector
- ❏ 4-in.-length of ½-in. copper tubing
- ❏ Hose clamps
- ❏ Wire connectors

DIFFICULTY LEVEL

This project can be completed in a day.

1 Start by shutting off the electrical power to the dishwasher circuit at the service panel. Also, turn off the water supply at the shutoff valve, usually located directly under the floor.

2 Remove the old unit. First unscrew the front access panel. Once the access panel is removed, disconnect the water supply line from the L-fitting on the bottom of the unit. This is usually a brass compression fitting, so just turning the compression nut counterclockwise with an adjustable wrench should do the trick. Use a bowl to catch any water that might leak out when the nut is removed.

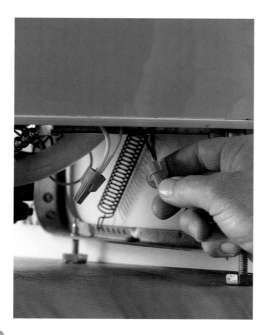

3 The dishwasher has an integral electrical box at the front of the unit where the power cable is attached to the dishwasher's fixture wires. Take off the box cover and remove the wire connectors that join the wires together.

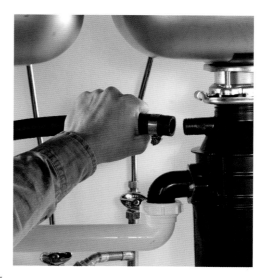

4 The discharge hose from the dishwasher is usually connected to the dishwasher port on the side of the garbage disposer. To remove it, just loosen the screw on the hose clamp and pull it off. You may need to push this hose back through a hole in the cabinet wall and into the dishwasher compartment so it won't get caught when you pull out the dishwasher.

5 The last thing that needs to be done before you can pull out the unit is to remove the screws that hold the brackets to the underside of the countertop. Then put a piece of cardboard or old carpet under the front legs, to protect the floor from getting scratched, and pull out the dishwasher.

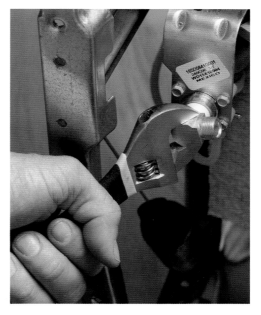

6 Tip the new dishwasher on its back and install the new L-fitting into the threaded port on the solenoid. Apply some Teflon tape or pipe sealant to the fitting threads before tightening it in place to prevent possible leaks.

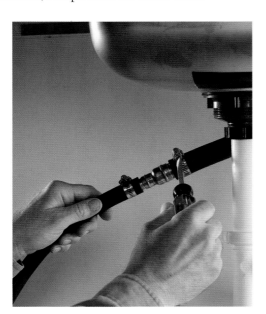

7 Attach a length of new automotive heater hose, usually ⅝" diameter, to the end of the dishwasher's discharge hose nipple with a hose clamp. The new hose you are adding should be long enough to reach from the discharge nipple to the port on the side of the kitchen sink garbage disposer.

8 Like the old dishwasher, the new one will have an integral electrical box for making the wiring connections. To gain access to the box, just remove the box cover. Then install a cable connector on the back of the box and bring the power cable from the service panel through this connector.

(Continued)

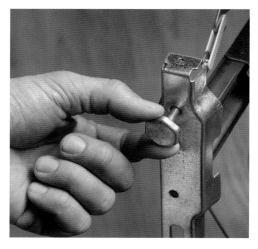

9 While the new dishwasher is still on its back, install a leveling leg at each of the four corners. Just turn these legs into the threaded holes designed for them. Leave about ½" of each leg projecting from the bottom of the unit. These will have to be adjusted later to keep the appliance level. Tip the appliance up onto these feet and push it into the opening. Check for level in both directions and adjust these feet as required.

10 Once the dishwasher is level, attach the brackets to the underside of the countertop to keep the appliance from moving. Then pull the discharge hose into the sink cabinet and install it so there's a loop that is attached with bracket to the underside of the countertop. This loop prevents waste water from flowing from the disposer back into the dishwasher.

LENGTHENING A DISCHARGE HOSE

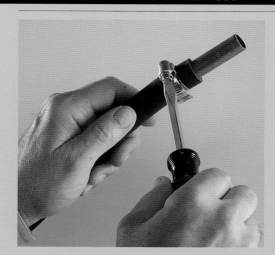

1 If the discharge hose has to be modified to fit onto the disposer port, first insert a 4"-long piece of ½" copper tubing into the hose and hold it in place with a hose clamp. This provides a nipple for the rubber adapter that fits onto the disposer.

2 Clamp the rubber disposer adapter to the end of the copper tubing nipple. Then tighten the hose clamp securely.

11 Push the adapter over the disposer's discharge nipple and tighten it in place with a hose clamp. If you don't have a disposer, this discharge hose can be clamped directly to a modified sink tailpiece that's installed below a standard sink strainer.

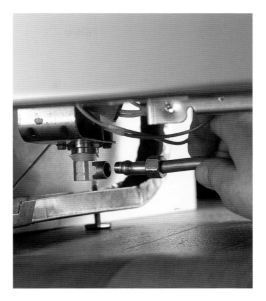

12 Adjust the L-fitting on the dishwasher's water inlet valve until it points directly toward the water supply tubing. Then lubricate the threads slightly with a drop of dishwashing liquid and tighten the tubing's compression nut onto the fitting. Use an adjustable wrench and turn the nut clockwise.

13 Complete the electrical connections by tightening the connector's clamp on the cable. Then join the power wires to the fixture wires with wire connectors, attach the ground wire (or wires) to the grounding screw on the box, and replace the cover.

14 Install the access panel, usually by hooking it on a couple of prongs just below the dishwasher's door. Install the screws that hold it in place and turn on the water and power supplies. Replace the toe-kick panel at the bottom of the dishwasher.

Water Heater

A WATER HEATER THAT LEAKS SHOULD BE REPLACED IMMEDIATELY TO PREVENT WATER DAMAGE.
Leaks normally occur because the inner tank has rusted through. When replacing an electric water heater, make sure the voltage of the new model is the same as the old heater. When replacing a gas water heater, maintain a clearance of 6" or more around the unit for ventilation. Water heaters are available with tank sizes ranging from 30 to 65 gallons. A 40- or 50-gallon heater should be large enough for a family of four.

Energy-efficient water heaters have polyurethane foam insulation and usually carry an extended warranty. These models are more expensive, but over the life of the water heater they cost less to operate. Tankless water heaters are available and may present a good replacement option (page 49).

The pressure-relief valve must usually be purchased separately. Make sure the new valve matches the working pressure rating of the tank.

INSTALL A WATER HEATER

DECODING NAMEPLATES

The nameplate on the water heater's side lists tank capacity, insulation R-value, and working pressure (pounds per square inch). More efficient water heaters have an insulation R-value of 7 or higher. The nameplate for an electric water heater includes the voltage and the wattage capacity of the heating elements and thermostats. Water heaters also have a yellow energy guide label that lists typical yearly operating costs. Estimates are based on national averages. Energy costs in your area may vary.

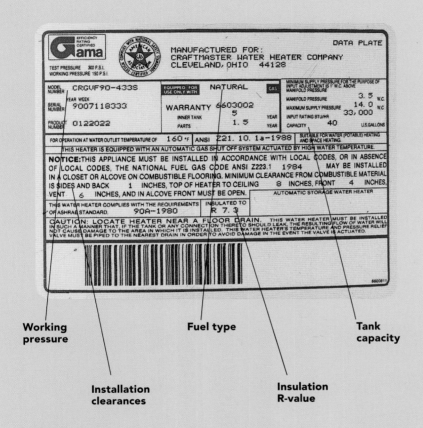

Working pressure

Installation clearances

Fuel type

Insulation R-value

Tank capacity

- ❏ Tape measure
- ❏ Reciprocating saw
- ❏ Drill
- ❏ Level
- ❏ 2" standpipe drain with trap
- ❏ 2" Y-fitting
- ❏ Waste tee fitting
- ❏ Pipe straps
- ❏ Solvent glue and primer
- ❏ 2½" deck screws
- ❏ ½" screws
- ❏ Hose bibs
- ❏ Two rubber supply hoses
- ❏ Teflon tape
- ❏ Recess mounted washing machine box

DIFFICULTY LEVEL

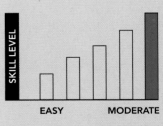

This project can be completed in a weekend.

1 Shut off the gas by turning the handle of the in-line valve so it is perpendicular to the gas line. Wait 10 minutes for gas to dissipate. Shut off the water supply at the shutoff valves.

2 Disconnect the gas line at the union fitting or at the flare fitting below the shutoff valve, using pipe wrenches. Disassemble and save the gas pipes and fittings.

3 Drain water from the water heater tank by opening the hose bib on the side of the tank. Drain the water into buckets, or attach a hose and empty the tank into a floor drain.

4 Disconnect the hot and cold water pipes above the water heater. If the pipes are soldered copper, use a hacksaw or tubing cutter to cut through the water pipes just a few inches below the shutoff valves. Cuts must be straight.

5 Disconnect the exhaust duct by removing the sheetmetal screws. Remove the old water heater with an appliance cart and dispose of it properly.

6 Position the new heater so that the control box is close to the gas line and the access panel for the burner chamber is not obstructed.

7 Level the water heater by driving wood shims under the legs.

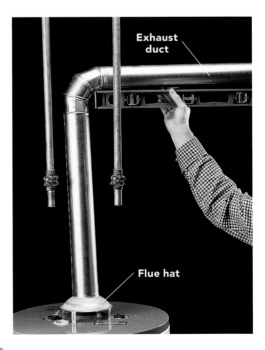

Exhaust duct

Flue hat

8 Position the flue hat so the legs fit into slots on the water heater, then slip the exhaust duct over the flue hat. Make sure horizontal duct slopes upward ¼" per ft. so fumes cannot back up into the house.

(Continued)

9 Attach the flue hat to the exhaust duct with three screws per joint.

10 Wrap the threads of the new pressure-relief valve (sold separately) with Teflon tape, and screw the valve into the tank opening with a pipe wrench.

11 Attach a copper or CPVC drain pipe to the pressure-relief valve, using a threaded male adapter. The pipe should reach to within 3" of the floor.

12 Solder threaded male adapters to the water supply pipes. Let the pipes cool, then wrap Teflon tape around the threads of the adapters.

13 Wrap Teflon tape around the threads of two heat-saver nipples. The nipples are color-coded, and have water-direction arrows to ensure proper installation.

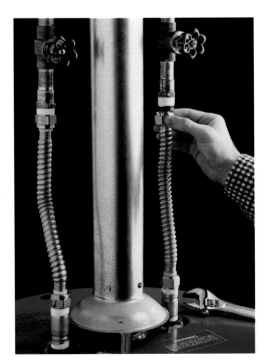

15 Connect the water lines to the heat-saver nipples with flexible water connectors. Tighten fittings with an adjustable wrench.

14 Attach the blue-coded nipple fitting to the cold water inlet and the red-coded fitting to the hot water outlet, using a pipe wrench. On the cold water nipple, the water direction arrow should face down; on the hot water nipple, the arrow should face up.

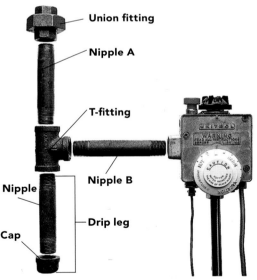

Union fitting

Nipple A

T-fitting

Nipple B

Nipple

Drip leg

Cap

16 Test-fit gas pipes and fittings from the old water heater. One or two new black-iron nipples (A, B) may by necessary if the new water heater is taller or shorter than the old heater. Use black iron, not galvanized iron, for gas lines. The capped nipple is called a drip leg. The drip leg protects the gas burner by catching dirt particles.

(Continued)

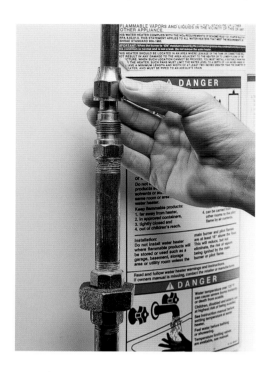

17 Clean pipe threads with a small wire brush, and coat the threads with pipe joint compound. Assemble gas line in the following order: control box nipple (1), T-fitting (2), vertical nipple (3), union fitting (4), vertical nipple (5), cap (6).

OPTION: If the gas line is made of flexible copper, use a flare fitting to connect the gas line to the water heater.

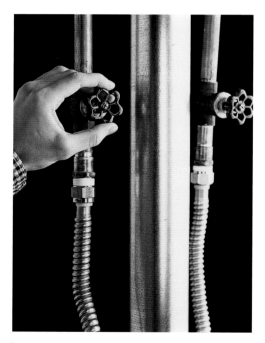

18 Open the hot water faucets throughout house, then open the water heater inlet and outlet shutoff valves. When water runs steadily, close the faucets.

19 Open the in-line valve on the gas line. Test for leaks by dabbing soapy water on each joint. Leaking gas will cause water to bubble. Tighten leaking joints with a pipe wrench.

20 Turn the gas cock on top of the control box to the PILOT position. Set the temperature control on the front of the box to the desired temperature.

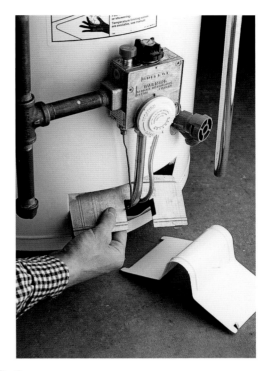

21 Remove the outer and inner access panels covering the burner chamber.

22 Light a match and hold flame next to the end of the pilot gas tube inside the burner chamber. Be sure to keep your face away from the opening.

23 While holding match next to end of pilot gas tube, press the reset button on top of the control box. When the pilot flame lights, continue to hold the reset button for one minute. Turn gas cock to ON position, and replace the inner and outer access panels.

1 Turn off power to water heater by switching off circuit breaker (or removing fuse) at the main service panel. Drain the water heater and disconnect the water pipes.

2 Drain water from the water heater tank by opening the hose bib on the side of the tank. Drain the water into buckets, or attach a hose and empty the tank into a floor drain.

3 Disconnect the hot and cold water pipes above the water heater. If the pipes are soldered copper, use a hacksaw or tubing cutter to cut through the water pipes just a few inches below the shutoff valves. Cuts must be straight.

4 Disconnect the exhaust duct by removing the sheetmetal screws.

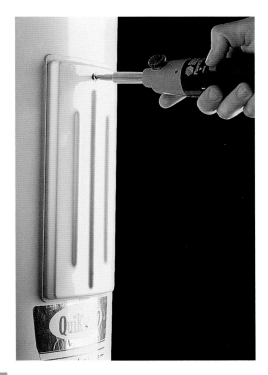

5 Remove one of the heating element access panels on the side of the old water heater.

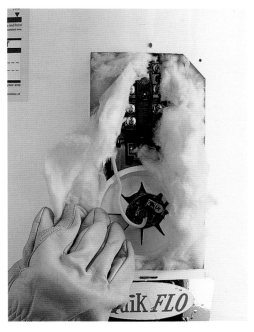

6 Wearing protective gloves, fold back the insulation to expose the thermostat. CAUTION: Do not touch bare wires until they have been tested for current.

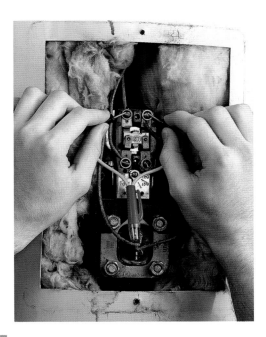

7 Test for current by touching probes of a circuit tester to the top pair of terminal screws on the thermostat. If the tester lights, wires are not safe to work on; turn off the main power switch and retest for current.

8 Remove the coverplate on the electrical box found at the side or top of the water heater. Disconnect all the wires, and label with masking tape for reference. Loosen the cable clamp and remove the wires by pulling them through the clamp. Remove the old heater, then position the new heater.

(Continued)

9 Connect the water pipes and pressure-relief valve, following directions for gas water heaters (page 42 to 43). Open the hot water faucets throughout the house and turn on the water. When water runs steadily, turn off the faucets.

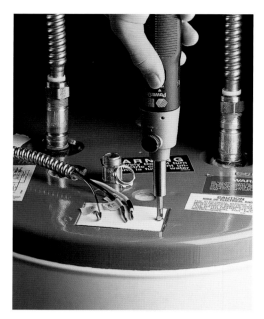

10 Remove the electrical box coverplate on the new water heater. Thread the circuit wires through the clamp. Thread the circuit wires through the cable opening on the water heater, and attach the clamp to the water heater.

11 Connect the circuit wires to the water heater wires, using wire connectors.

12 Attach the bare copper or green ground wire to the ground screw. Replace the coverplate.

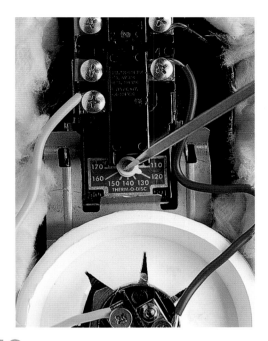

13 Remove the access panels on the side of the water heater, and use a screwdriver to set the thermostat to the desired water temperature (120° to 130° F).

14 Press the reset button on the thermostat. Replace the insulation and access panels. Turn on the power and test.

TANKLESS WATER HEATERS

Common in Europe for generations, gas-fueled on-demand water heaters are increasing in popularity in North America. Because they do not require a tank, they heat only the water you need, as you need it. This is a great improvement in efficiency over continually heating a tank with 40 or 50 gallons of water in it. But on the down side, tankless heaters may not be able to keep up with your hot water demands if you are using multiple fixtures, and they are still at least three times as costly as gas or electric water heaters when installed by a professional.

Water Softener

IF YOUR HOUSE HAS HARD WATER COURSING THROUGH ITS PIPES, THEN YOU'VE GOT A COUPLE OF problems. Not only does your water do a poor job of dissolving soap, but you also have plenty of scale deposits on dishes, plumbing fixtures, and the inside of your water heater.

Softeners fix these problems by chemically removing the calcium and magnesium that are responsible for the hard water (usually described as over 18 grains of minerals per gallon). These units are installed after the water meter but before the water line branches off to appliances or fixtures, with one exception: Piping to outside faucets should branch off the main line before the softener because treating outside water is a waste of money.

Softeners come with an overflow tube and a purge tube to rinse out the minerals that are extracted from the water. These tubes should be attached to the floor drain or to a laundry sink basin, which is the better approach if the sink is close by.

INSTALL A WATER SOFTENER

SOFTENED WATER

From your plumbing's point of view, the best water softening strategy is to position the softener close to the main, cold-only supply line (as seen here). Doing this results in both hot and cold water being softened. But because some homeowners object to the altered taste and increased salinity of softened water, the softener may be installed after the hot and cold lines have split from the main supply line. This way, the water may be softened immediately before it enters the heater, and the cold water remains unsoftened.

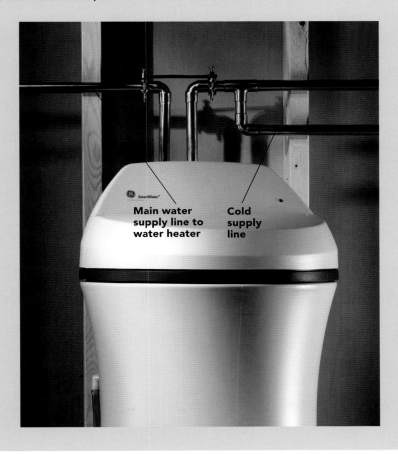

Main water supply line to water heater

Cold supply line

KNOW YOUR TYPES OF SALT

Salt for water softeners comes in three basic types: rock salt, solar salt (crystals) and evaporated salt (pellets). Rock salt is a mineral that's mined from salt deposits. Solar salt is a crystalline residue left behind when seawater is evaporated naturally. It sometimes is sold as pellets or blocks. Evaporated salt is similar to solar salt, but the liquid in the brine is evaporated using mechanical methods. Rock salt is cheapest but leaves behind the most residue and therefore requires more frequent brine tank cleaning. Evaporated salt pellets are the cleanest and require the least maintenance.

TOOLS & MATERIALS YOU NEED

❑ Tape measure
❑ Tubing cutter
❑ Propane torch
❑ Slip-joint pliers
❑ Steel wool
❑ Soldering flux
❑ Solder
❑ 4"-thick concrete blocks

DIFFICULTY LEVEL

SKILL LEVEL

EASY · MODERATE

This project can be completed in a weekend.

1 The first step is to measure the distance between the bypass ports on the tank to the cold water supply line. Cut copper tubing to fit this space and solder appropriate fittings onto both ends.

2 Following the manufacturer's directions, install the plastic tubing discharge tube on the head of the water softener.

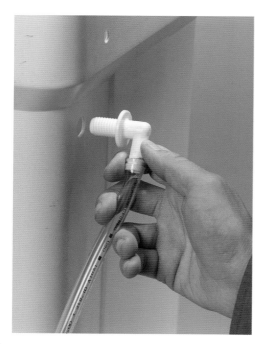

3 The overflow tube is usually connected to the side of the softener's tank. Run this tube, along with the discharge tube, to a floor drain or a laundry sink.

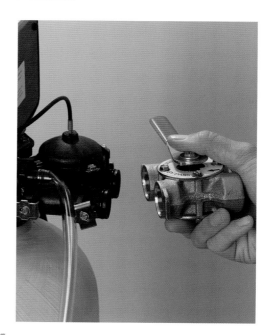

4 Install the code-required bypass valve in the softener's head. One side of the valve goes in the inlet port and the other fits into the outlet port. This valve is held in place with simple plastic clips or threaded couplings.

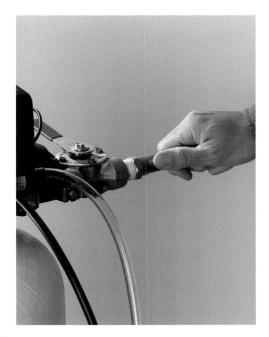

5 Attach the copper tubing that supplies the water to the bypass valve. For this unit, the joint is made with a male threaded union that screws onto the bypass valve ports.

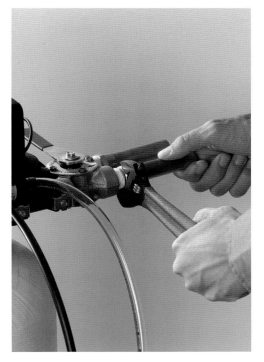

6 Tighten both supply tube nuts with a wrench. Do not over-tighten them.

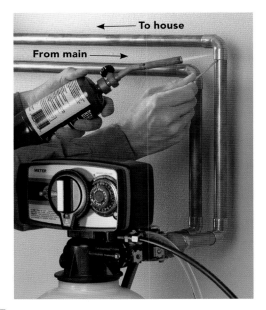

← To house

From main →

7 Connect the copper tubing from the softener to the water supply lines. Clean all fittings and pipes with steel wool. Then, apply soldering flux to the parts and solder them together with a propane torch. For more information on soldering copper, consult a plumbing manual.

8 Turn on the water supply and make sure the installation works properly. If you see any leaks, fix them. Then add the water softening pellets to the top of the unit in the ratios explained on the package.

Range Hood

RANGE HOODS DO MORE THAN JUST GET RID OF COOKING ODORS. THEIR MOST IMPORTANT JOB is to reduce the amount of water vapor in the air that's generated by routine cooking. The pot of water that boils for 30 minutes before you remember to drop in the pasta adds a lot of water vapor into your house. Usually the results are innocent enough. But prolonged periods of high moisture can lead to mildew and other molds that can stain your walls and ceilings and possibly make family members sick.

The hardest part of adding a range hood is installing the ductwork between the hood and the outside of your house. If the range is located on an outside wall, the best choice is to run the duct from the back of the hood straight through the wall. If you have wood siding, this job is not difficult. But if you have brick or stone, plan on spending several hours to cut this hole.

If the range is on an interior wall, the preferred route is usually from the top of the hood through the roof. It's also possible to put the duct into the attic, then across the ceiling (between two rafters or trusses) and out through an overhanging soffit.

INSTALL A RANGE HOOD

VENT HOOD TYPES

A traditional range hood like the one installed for this project fits into the upper cabinet network, usually with the ductwork hidden behind cabinet doors (bottom photo). If this type of range hood is not practical for your situation (for instance, if your cooktop is in an island) install a downdraft vent (top photo).

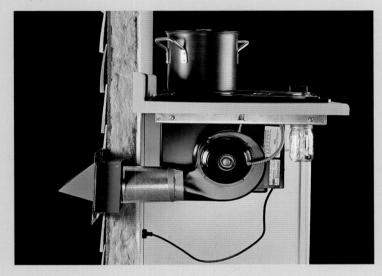

TERMS YOU'LL NEED TO KNOW

45° ADJUSTABLE ELBOWS—Made of galvanized steel to prevent corrosion, these adjustable fittings are used to join ducts at angles. When paired together, they can form nearly any angle from 0° to 90°.

TOOLS & MATERIALS YOU NEED

- ❏ Hammer
- ❏ Jig saw
- ❏ Multipurpose tool
- ❏ Screwdrivers
- ❏ Electric drill and bits
- ❏ Utility knife
- ❏ Circular Saw
- ❏ Caulking gun
- ❏ Screws
- ❏ Wire connectors
- ❏ Sheet metal screws
- ❏ Duct tape
- ❏ Range hood and duct work
- ❏ Weatherproof roof cap or weatherproof wall cap
- ❏ Plastic roof cement

DIFFICULTY LEVEL

SKILL LEVEL

EASY   MODERATE

This project can be completed in a weekend.

1 Install the vent duct in the wall first, then cut a hole in the back of the range hood cabinet and mount the cabinet over the duct. Cut a vent hole in the bottom of the cabinet to match the opening on the top of the hood.

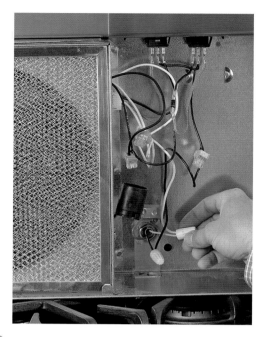

2 Make sure the circuit power is turned off at the service panel, then join the power cable wires to the lead wires inside the range hood. Use wire connectors for this job.

3 Get someone to help lift the range hood into place and hold it there while you attach it. Drive two screws through both sides and into the adjacent cabinets. If the hood is slightly small for the opening, slip a shim between the hood and the walls, trying to keep the gaps even.

4 Run ductwork from the cabinet to the exhaust exit point. Use two 45° adjustable elbows to join the duct in the wall to the top of the range hood. Use sheet metal screws and duct tape to hold all parts together and keep them from moving.

ALTERNATIVE: Install a downdraft cooktop with a built-in blower unit that vents through the back or bottom of a base cabinet. A downdraft cooktop is a good choice for a kitchen island or peninsula.

WALL VENT: If the duct comes out through the sidewall of the house, install a vertical duct cap. Make sure to seal around the perimeter of the cap with exterior caulk.

CEILING VENT: If the duct goes through an overhang soffit, you'll need a transition fitting to connect the round duct to a short piece of rectangular duct. Once these parts are installed, add a protective grille to keep animals and insects from getting into the duct.

ROOF VENT: For ducts that pass through the roof, cut an access hole through the roofing and sheathing, then install a weatherproof cap on top of the duct and under the roofing shingles. Make a waterproof seal by caulking the cap with plastic roof cement. If you don't have much roofing experience, consult a roofing manual for some more information on this step.

Hot Water Dispenser

IT'S STILL EASY TO FIND A REFRIGERATOR WITHOUT A COLD WATER DISPENSER IN ITS DOOR, BUT you have to walk past a lot of product before you see one. This says something about people liking convenience. In many ways, a hot water dispenser is even more convenient than a cold water dispenser. There are boxes and boxes of beverages and food that need only a trickle of hot water to achieve their destiny: coffee, tea, hot chocolate, instant soup, hot cereals, and just plain old hot water and lemon to name a few. And there's no faster way to get this hot water than with a hot water dispenser. These units are designed to fit in the spare hole on many kitchen sink decks. But, if you don't have one, you can replace your spray hose with the dispenser. Or, if you want to keep the hose, just drill an extra hole in your sink or countertop to accommodate the dispenser faucet.

NOTE: Installing this appliance requires both plumbing and wiring work. If you are unsure of your skills in these areas, hire a professional. (Be sure to check your local codes before starting.)

INSTALL A HOT WATER DISPENSER

SWITCHED RECEPTACLE

Three wires are connected to the switch/receptacle. One of the hot wires is the feed wire that brings power into the box. It is connected to the side of the switch that has a connecting tab. The other hot wire carries power out to the light fixture or appliance. It is connected to the brass screw terminal on the side that does not have a connecting tab. The white neutral wire is pigtailed to the silver screw terminal. The grounding wires must be pigtailed to the green grounding screw on the switch/receptacle and to the grounded metal box.

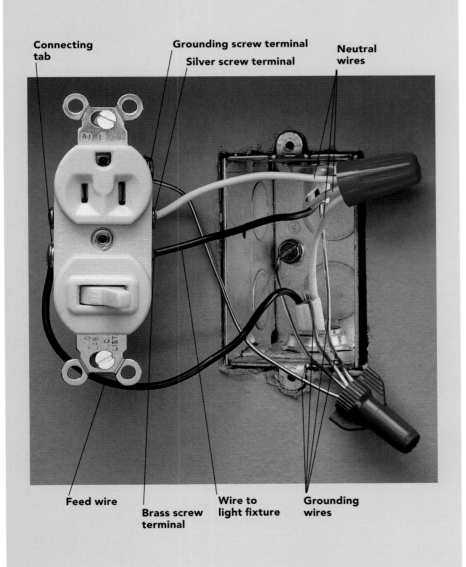

Connecting tab

Grounding screw terminal

Silver screw terminal

Neutral wires

Feed wire

Brass screw terminal

Wire to light fixture

Grounding wires

DIFFICULTY LEVEL

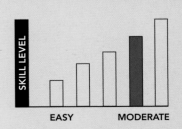

This project can be completed in a weekend.

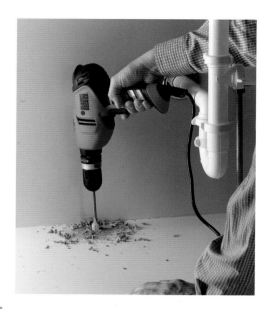

1 Drill an access hole for new power cable (in flexible conduit) in the bottom of the sink compartment cabinet. Use a drill and a ¾"-dia. bit. Go into the basement and drill a hole up through the flooring that will align with the first hole. (Or make other arrangements to run circuit wire as you see fit.)

2 Fish a 14/2 cable from the electric service panel up through the hole in the floor. Strip the sheathing from the cable with a utility knife. Also strip the insulation from the wires with a wire stripper. Do not nick the wire insulation.

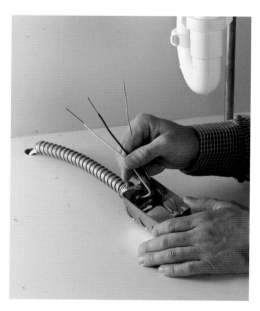

3 Cut a piece of flexible conduit and slide it over the cable, so the cable is protected from the point it leaves the cabinet floor to when it enters the electrical box. Attach the conduit to the box with a box connector so at least 8" of wire reaches into the box.

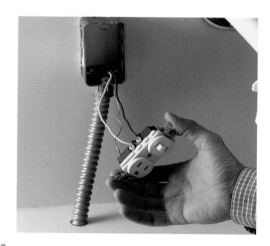

4 To conform to code, we installed a switched receptacle. Mount a duplex metal box on the cabinet wall. Connect the black power wire to the brass screw on the switch. Attach the white neutral wire to the silver screw on the receptacle. Run a short black jumper wire from the second switch terminal to the brass terminal screw on the receptacle. Attach the ground wire to the receptacle ground screw and the box ground screw, using pigtail connections.

5 The water supply to the dispenser comes from the cold water supply line under the kitchen sink. Mount a tee on this pipe, below its shutoff valve, by alternately tightening the tee bolts on both sides with a wrench.

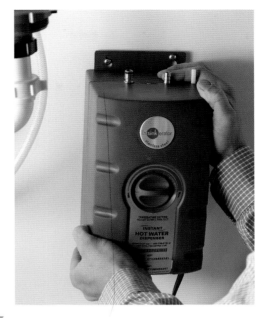

6 Determine the best place for the dispenser heater, usually on the back cabinet wall, so its pigtail plug will reach the switched receptacle. Screw its mounting bracket to the wall and hang the heater on this bracket.

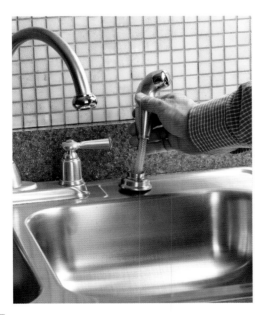

7 To replace a spray hose with the dispenser faucet, remove the nut that holds the sprayer to the sink. Then remove the end of the hose from its port on the bottom of the faucet, using an adjustable wrench. This will free the hose so it can be pulled out from above the sink.

8 The faucet port for the spray hose must be closed after the hose is removed. To do this, buy a plug at a hardware store or a plumbing supply store. Then cover its threads with Teflon tape, turn it into the port and then tighten with an adjustable wrench.

(Continued)

9 The dispenser faucet is designed to fit into a standard sink hole. To install it, just squeeze its supply tubes together so they can fit into the hole, and drop it in place. The unit is held securely by a washer and locking screw that is tightened from below the sink.

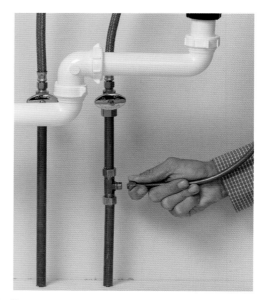

10 The faucet is joined to the sink supply tee with a piece of flexible tubing. Measure this piece, make the cut with a tubing cutter, and install compression nuts and ferrules on both ends. Slide one end of the tubing into the valve and tighten the nut with a wrench.

11 On the model seen here, the heater unit has three tubes. One supplies cold water to the heater, one supplies hot water to the faucet, and a third clear plastic hose acts as a vent and is attached to an expansion tank within the heater. Attach the two copper water tubes to the heater with compression fittings. Tighten them with a wrench.

12 Slide the end of the plastic vent tube onto the copper nipple on top of the tank and attach it according to the manufacturer's instructions. On some models a spring clip is used for this job, other models require a hose clamp.

13 To install the heater power supply cable in the service panel, begin by turning off the main power breaker. Then remove the outside door panel and remove one of the knockout plates from the top or side of the box. Install a cable clamp inside this hole, push the cable through the clamp, and tighten the clamp to secure the cable.

14 Strip the sheathing from the cable inside the panel and remove the insulation from the ends on the black and white cable wires. Loosen two lug screws on the neutral/grounding bus bar and push the white wire under one lug and the ground wire under the other lug. Tighten both these screws securely.

15 Loosen the lug screw on a standard 15-amp breaker and put the end of the black (hot) cable wire under this lug. Tighten the lug with a screwdriver. Then install the breaker in the hot bus bar by pushing it into place.

16 Once a new breaker is installed, the service panel cover has to be modified to fit over it. To do this, break out the protective plate that covers the breaker position with pliers. Then lift up the cover, screw it to the panel, and turn on the main breaker. Turn on the water supply to the dispenser system and plug the dispenser heater into the receptacle. Turn on the receptacle switch, wait fifteen minutes, and check that the system is working properly.

Icemaker

MOST EXPENSIVE REFRIGERATORS COME WITH ICEMAKERS AS STANDARD EQUIPMENT, and practically every model features them as an option (a refrigerator with an icemaker usually costs about $100 more). It is also possible to purchase an icemaker as a retrofit feature for your old fridge. Installing one is a pretty simple job, especially if you buy a kit made by the same manufacturer that built your refrigerator. Most appliance stores can look up the information for you (be sure to bring your model number along) to make certain you get the right product.

If you are using equipment from the same manufacturer, things should fit properly and the job becomes a straightforward assembly project. The screws that come in the kit fit the holes in the refrigerator. The hardest part is running water from a convenient supply line. Because you are working in the kitchen, one sensible source is the cold water line under the kitchen sink. But often, by drilling a small hole in the floor, you can access a nearby line in the basement without having to fish your tubing behind (or through) a bank of cabinets.

INSTALL AN ICEMAKER

AFTERMARKET ICEMAKERS

Most icemakers either come preinstalled or are purchased as an accessory when you buy your new refrigerator. But if you have an older refrigerator with no icemaker and you'd like it to have one, all is not lost. Inspect the back of the unit, behind the freezer compartment. If your refrigerator has the required plumbing to support an icemaker you will see a port or a port that is covered with backing. In that case, all you need to do is take the make and model information to an appliance parts dealer and they can sell you an aftermarket icemaker. Plan to spend $100 to $200.

HOW ICEMAKERS WORK

An icemaker receives its supply of water for making cubes through a ¼" copper supply line that runs from the icemaker to a water pipe. The supply line runs through a valve in the refrigerator and is controlled by a solenoid that monitors the water supply and sends the water into the icemaker itself, where it is turned into ice cubes. The cubes drop down into a bin and as their level rises they also raise a bail wire that's connected to a shutoff. When the bin is full, the bail wire will be high enough to trigger a mechanism that shuts off the water supply.

TERMS YOU'LL NEED TO KNOW

SOLENOID—A plunger valve that is usually opened by an electric coil and closed by the actions of a spring, gravity, or a second electric coil terminal; often used to control the flow of liquids.

TOOLS & MATERIALS YOU NEED

❏ Screwdrivers
❏ Nut drivers
❏ Needle-nose pliers
❏ Duct or masking tape
❏ Electric drill and assorted bits
❏ Channel-type pliers
❏ Open-end wrenches or an adjustable wrench
❏ Icemaker kit
❏ Saddle valve or T-fitting (for supply tube)

DIFFICULTY LEVEL

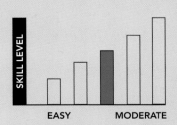

This project can be completed in a weekend.

HOW TO INSTALL AN ICEMAKER

1 Begin work by reviewing the installation instructions that came with your icemaker kit. While most kits are very similar, there are some differences between models. Remove all the contents from the refrigerator and freezer compartments and store them in ice chests or in a neighbor's refrigerator. Unplug the unit and pull it out from the wall. Then open the freezer door and remove the icemaker cover plate at the back of the compartment.

2 On the back side of the refrigerator, remove the backing or unscrew the icemaker access panel that covers the icemaker port.

3 Once the backing or access panel is removed, you'll find two openings. One opening is for the water line. The other is for a wiring harness. Usually, these holes are filled with insulation plugs that keep the cold air inside the freezer from leaking out into the room. Remove these plugs with needle-nose pliers.

4 Install the water tube assembly (part of the icemaker kit) in its access hole on the back of the refrigerator. This assembly features a plastic elbow attached to the plastic tube that reaches into the freezer compartment.

5 Icemaker kits usually come with a wiring harness that joins the icemaker motor inside the freezer box to the power supply wires installed on the back of the refrigerator. Push this harness through its access hole and into the freezer compartment. Then seal the hole with the plastic grommet that comes with the harness.

6 Join the end of the icemaker wiring harness to the power connector that was preinstalled on the back of the refrigerator. This connection should lay flat against the back. If it doesn't, just tape it down with some duct tape or masking tape.

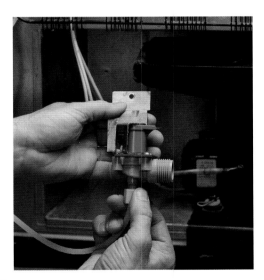

7 The water tube at the top of the refrigerator is attached to the solenoid that is mounted at the bottom with a plastic water line. To install the line, first attach it to the water tube, then run it down the back of the refrigerator and attach it to the solenoid valve with a compression fitting. This job is easier to do before you attach the solenoid assembly to the refrigerator cabinet.

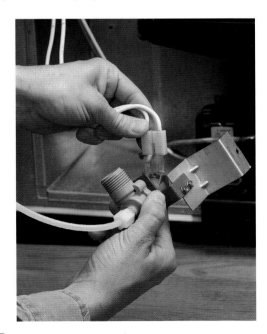

8 The icemaker wiring harness comes with two snap connectors. One goes to the preinstalled wires on the refrigerator and the other is attached to the solenoid. Just push this second connector onto the brass tabs, usually at the top of the solenoid.

(Continued)

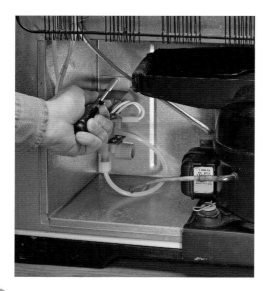

9 The solenoid is attached to a mounting bracket that should be installed on the cabinet wall at the bottom of the refrigerator. Mounting holes may be predrilled in the cabinet for this purpose. But if not, drill holes to match the bracket and the size of the screws. Then attach the bracket and make sure to attach the solenoid ground wire to one of these screws.

10 Once the solenoid is mounted, install the water-inlet copper tube. Attach it by tightening the nut on one end with channel-type pliers. The other end of the tube is held to the refrigerator cabinet with a simple clamp. Make sure the end of this tubing is pointing straight up.

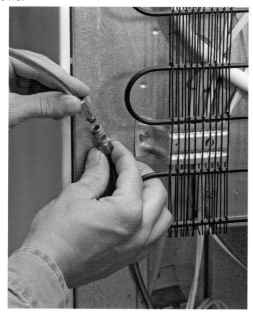

11 The end of the water-inlet tube is joined to the water supply tubing (from the house plumbing system) with a brass compression coupling. Tighten the compression nuts with an open-end or adjustable wrench.

12 Run the water tubing to the kitchen sink cabinet or through the floor to a cold water pipe below. Turn off the water supply at the nearest shutoff valve. Install a saddle valve over the pipe and tighten both sides with the screws. Attach the icemaker tubing to the valve with a compression fitting. Turn the valve handle clockwise until it pierces the pipe; then turn the handle out to let the water go into the tubing.

13 From inside the freezer compartment, make sure the water tube and the wiring harness (from the back of the refrigerator) are free. If they are caught on the cabinet, loosen them until they are easily accessible.

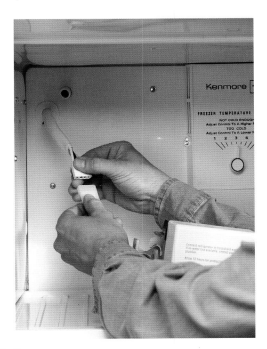

14 Join the wiring connector on the back of the icemaker to the connector on the end of the wiring harness. These connectors join in only one way, so it's impossible to cross the connectors.

15 Join the water supply tube to the back of the icemaker with a spring clip or a hose clamp. Then remove any small rubber caps that may be installed in the mounting screw holes, with a narrow putty knife. Lift the unit and screw it to the freezer wall. The mounting bracket holes are usually slotted to permit leveling the unit. Plug in the refrigerator and test the icemaker.

Reverse Osmosis Water Filter

NOT ALL WATER IS CREATED EQUAL. SOME WATER TASTES BETTER THAN OTHER WATER. SOME water looks better than other water. And some has more impurities, too. Because no one wants to drink bad water, the bottled water business has exploded over the past twenty years. Home filtration systems have also grown by leaps and bounds, in part because there are so many different types of filters available.

For example, sediment filters will remove rust, sand, and suspended minerals, like iron. A carbon filter can remove residual chlorine odors, some pesticides and even radon gas. Distillation filters can remove bacteria and organic compounds, while a traditional water softener can neutralize hard water. But many of the most toxic impurities, heavy metals like mercury, lead, cadmium, and arsenic, are best removed with a reverse-osmosis (RO) system like the one shown here.

These filters are designed to treat just cooking and drinking water. The system holds the treated water in a storage tank and delivers it to a sink-mounted faucet on demand. RO units feature multiple filter cartridges; in this case a pre-filter unit, followed by the RO membrane, followed by a carbon post-filter.

INSTALL A REVERSE OSMOSIS WATER FILTER

POINT-OF-USE FILTERS

Point-of-use water filtration systems typically are installed in the sink base cabinet, with a separate faucet from the main kitchen faucet. The setup shown here has an extra filter to supply a nearby refrigerator icemaker.

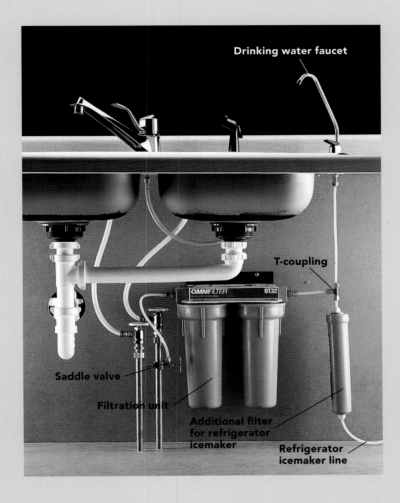

Drinking water faucet

T-coupling

Saddle valve

Filtration unit

Additional filter for refrigerator icemaker

Refrigerator icemaker line

TERMS YOU'LL NEED TO KNOW

REVERSE OSMOSIS—A water filtration system that works in concert with other filter mediums to purify drinking water. Its primary component is a dense, semi-permeable membrane that will allow water molecules to pass through, but will block impurities.

DIFFICULTY LEVEL

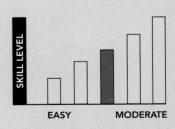

SKILL LEVEL

EASY   MODERATE

This project can be completed in a weekend.

1 The RO membrane filter is shipped in a separate bag that is filled with anti-bacterial fluid. Wearing plastic gloves, remove the cartridge from the bag and install it in the filter unit. Make sure to touch only the ends of the cartridge when you handle it or you can damage the membrane.

2 Following the manufacturer's instructions, establish the best location for the filter inside your kitchen sink cabinet. Then drive some mounting screws in the cabinet wall to support the unit.

3 Assemble the entire filtration system and then hang it on the cabinet wall. The best system layout may be to locate the filter on one wall and the storage tank on the opposite wall.

4 The side of the storage tank has to be outfitted with a simple valve. To install it, just wrap its threads a couple of times with Teflon tape and screw the valve into the tank. Finger-tighten it, then turn it one more turn with an adjustable wrench.

5 The filter is connected to the tank with plastic tubing. In most units, the joint between the two is made with a compression fitting. On this filter, the fitting is a push-type collar. Simply insert the hose into the collar until it will not go any farther.

6 The water storage tank and faucet are connected with plastic tubing. Here, a push-type compression fitting on the end of the tubing was used. To install it, push the end of the fitting over the bottom of the faucet shank until the fitting bottoms out.

7 The filter faucet comes with a jamb nut and sometimes a plastic spacer (as with this unit) that goes on the shank of the faucet before the jamb nut. After the nut is finger tight, snug it securely with an adjustable wrench. This unit came with a C-shaped collar and jamb nut, but a round collar would need to have hoses threaded through it prior to mounting the faucet.

8 Remove the cover from an unused sink hole, or remove the spray hose (see page 61), or bore a mounting-hole in the sink or into the countertop. Once you have prepared a suitable hole for the faucet stem, insert it from above.

(Continued)

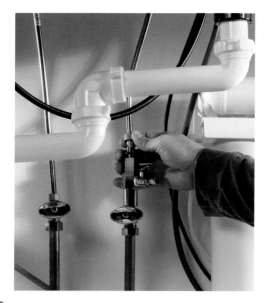

9 The water supply to the filter comes from the cold-water supply line that services the kitchen sink faucet. The easiest way to tap into the supply line is to replace the shutoff valve at the supply riser with a new valve containing an additional outlet for tubing.

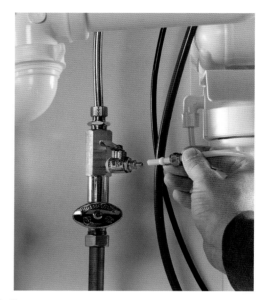

10 Attach the filter supply tube to the port on the shut-off valve with a compression fitting. Push the end of the tubing onto the valve, then push the ferrule against the valve and thread the compression nut into place. Finger tighten it, then turn it one more full turn with a wrench.

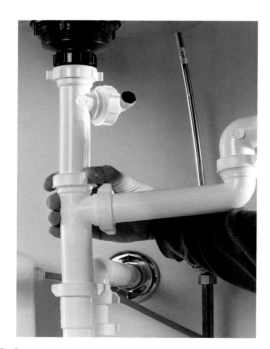

11 The filter must also be tied into the drain system. The best way to do this is to replace the drain tailpiece with a new fitting that contains an auxiliary port.

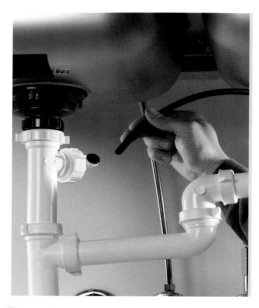

12 Attach the tubing from the drain to the auxiliary port on the tailpiece. Finish up by turning on the water and checking the system for leaks. Be sure to filter and drain at least two tanks of water, to clean any contaminants from the system, before drinking the water.

INSTALLING A WHOLE-HOUSE WATER FILTRATION SYSTEM

A whole-house water filtration system is installed along the supply pipe carrying water to the house, located after the water meter, but before any other appliances in the pipe line. A whole-house system reduces the same elements as an undersink system and can also help reduce the iron flowing into the water softener, prolonging its life.

Always follow the manufacturer's directions for your particular unit. If your electrical system is grounded through the water pipes, make sure to install ground clamps on both sides of the filtration unit with a connecting jumper wire. Globe valves should be installed within 6" of the intake and the outtake sides of the filter.

Filters must be replaced every few months, depending on type of manufacturer. The filtration unit cover unscrews for filter access.

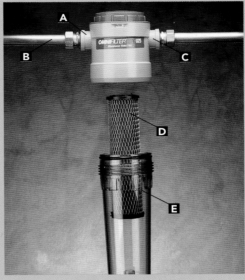

A WHOLE-HOUSE WATER FILTRATION SYSTEM: intake side (A), supply pipe from the water meter pipe (B), outtake side to the house supply pipe (C), filter (D), and filtration unit cover (E).

1 Shut off main water supply and turn on faucets to drain pipes. Position unit after water meter, but before any other appliances in supply pipe. Measure and mark pipe to accomodate the filtration unit. Cut pipe at marks with a pipe cutter. Join water meter side of pipe with intake side of unit, and house supply side of pipe with outtake side of unit. Tighten with a wrench.

2 Install a filter and screw filtration unit cover to bottom of the filtration unit. Attach a jumper wire to pipes on other side of unit, using pipe clamps. Open main water supply lines to restore the water supply. Allow faucets to run for a few minutes, as you check to make sure that the system is working properly.

Room Air Conditioner

IN TEMPERATE CLIMATES, WINDOW AIR CONDITIONERS CAN SOLVE JUST ABOUT EVERYONE'S cooling needs. That's the good news. The not-so-good news is that room air conditioners are usually installed in windows and, as a result, they greatly reduce the view you can enjoy. Window-installed units also present a much greater security risk. In a non-reinforced installation even a person of moderate strength can pull the unit out of the window with ease.

An alternative to a window unit is to install a wall-mounted air conditioner. Although these function just like room models, they are installed in sleeves that are permanently mounted in the wall, which means you don't have to install and remove them seasonally.

The mounting sleeve is tailored to fit a specific air conditioner unit, and the sleeve and appliance are normally purchased together as a set. This means your choices will be fairly limited when installing a through-the-wall model, compared to a window-mount model. Do not use a window unit in a through-the-wall installation.

INSTALL A ROOM AIR CONDITIONER

CIRCUIT REQUIREMENTS

Window air conditioners are considered permanent appliances when calculating electrical load. Most codes stipulate that they should have a dedicated 15-amp or 20-amp circuit. To learn how much amperage and wattage your air conditioner draws, look for a name plate, usually located on the top of the housing unit.

TERMS YOU'LL NEED TO KNOW

POP RIVETS—Small pins made of malleable metal that have a wide head on one end. Used to join two thin (usually sheet metal) parts. The rivet is first pushed into a predrilled hole in the mating parts. Then it is squeezed with a pop rivet tool. This causes the underside of the rivet to spread out and squeeze the mating parts against the rivet head.

DIFFICULTY LEVEL

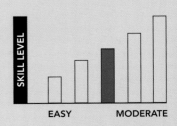

This project can be completed in a weekend.

HOW TO INSTALL A ROOM AIR CONDITIONER

1 Remove the through-the-wall sleeve and measure for the required opening. Establish the best location for the air conditioner, taking into consideration comfortable operating height on the interior (the closer they are to the ceiling the more efficiently they work). Outline the sleeve on the wall using a level as a guide.

2 Determine the location of the wall studs in the area you've chosen for the unit. An electronic stud finder is a good tool for this job. Mark where the studs fall. **NOTE:** If you are installing the unit in a load-bearing wall, be sure to supply temporary support and install an approved header in the opening. Ask your local building department.

3 Remove the drywall and wall insulation from the area where the sleeve will go. Remove drywall at least 16" beyond the sleeve limits so you'll have room to modify the wall framing. Mark the location of the sleeve on the framing members. It's easiest if you use an existing stud as one end of the opening.

4 Cut out the sections of wall studs that fall within the installation area. You can do this with a handsaw. But the best tool for the job is a reciprocating saw. It's an inexpensive rental tool item and is designed specifically for this type of work. Once the studs are cut, pry out the waste with a flat pry bar.

5 Install cripple studs next to the full studs on both ends of the opening to support the rough sill. Cut these cripple studs to the same length as the cut studs (if next to one) and nail them into the full studs and toenail them into the bottom wall plate.

6 Cut the rough sill from the same size framing lumber as is in the wall. It should fit between the full studs on both sides of the opening. Nail it to the cut studs. Install the head framing member, then add cripple studs at the ends of the opening (allow for their thickness when planning the opening). Check this opening for square, and drive shims behind the frame members, if necessary.

7 To mark the sleeve opening on the outside of the house, drill a hole through the exterior wall sheathing in all four corners of the framed opening. A ¼"-dia. bit usually does the trick.

8 Draw lines between the corner holes on the outside of the house. Then, install an old blade in a circular saw and set the blade depth to match the thickness of the siding and sheathing plus about ½". Starting at one corner, carefully make a plunge cut into the siding and continue up until you reach the next corner. Finish the cuts at the corners with a handsaw or jig saw.

(Continued)

9 Once the siding and sheathing have been removed, slide the air conditioner sleeve into the opening and position it according to the manufacturer's instructions. When it's aligned properly, attach it to the wall opening frame with screws driven through the side panels of the sleeve (first drill clearance holes).

10 After the sleeve is installed, the top has to be covered with flashing to fend off leaks. The first step is to cut a piece of metal flashing to slightly longer than the width of the sleeve. Fold it into a 90° angle, then work one side under the siding at the top of the opening. Drill a pop rivet hole through the flashing and into the sleeve every 4" across the entire width.

11 Once the holes are drilled, lift up the flashing and run a heavy bead of silicone caulk between the flashing and sleeve. Make sure that the caulk is applied in a continuous, unbroken bead so that no water can seep past it.

12 Push the flashing into the caulk and hold it flat next to each hole. Install a pop rivet in each hole with a pop rivet gun. When all the rivets are installed, wipe away any excess caulk that squeezed out of the joint.

13 The entire perimeter of the sleeve needs to be sealed with caulk. Use silicone caulk, and make sure to apply a particularly heavy bead where the flashing meets the siding above the unit. Also cover the tops of the rivets so they won't leak.

14 If there is any space between the sleeve and the rough framing, fill it with fiberglass insulation or expandable spray foam. Just take some thin pieces of insulation and push them into these spaces with a screwdriver or putty knife. Also replace the insulation and vapor retarder in the stud cavities.

15 Cut drywall strips to fit around the sleeve frame, and nail or screw them to the wall framing. Once all the drywall is installed, finish it with joint compound and drywall tape. When the drywall finishing is done, prime and paint the wall.

16 Slide the air conditioner into the sleeve and attach the front cover. Plug in the power cord and turn on the unit to make sure it works properly. If you must use an extension cord, buy an appliance-rated cord that's as short as possible for your needs.

Thermostat

TRADITIONAL FURNACE THERMOSTATS ARE LOW-VOLTAGE MODELS THAT DO A SIMPLE, BUT necessary, job. They sense changes in the house air temperature and when it's too low, the thermostat turns on the heat and when it's too high, the thermostat turns off the heat. For many years this was all we needed to make our homes comfortable and no one gave much thought to improving this performance. Then, fuel shortages and high energy costs made everyone interested in lowering the heating fuel bill.

One innovation that has advanced this effort is the programmable thermostat. This provided more control over furnaces and, as a result, reduced energy consumption. If everyone in the house is gone during the day, there's no reason to keep the heat at 68 or 70 degrees or more. And when everyone goes to sleep at night, these thermostats turn down the heat automatically and turn it back on before anyone gets up. Different models that offer different levels of control are available. Generally, the more capability a unit has, the more it costs. While there is variety in what the units can do, most are easy to install, as shown here.

UPGRADE A THERMOSTAT

PROGRAMMABLE THERMOSTATS

Programmable thermostats contain sophisticated circuitry that allows you to set the heating and cooling systems in your house to adjust automatically at set times of day. Replacing a manual thermostat with a programmable model is a relatively simple job that can have big payback on heating and cooling energy savings.

CHECK BEFORE YOU BUY

When buying a new thermostat, make sure the new unit is compatible with your heating/air conditioning system. For reference, bring the brand names and model numbers of the old thermostat, the furnace, and the central air conditioning unit to the store and provide the information to the sales assistant.

TERMS YOU'LL NEED TO KNOW

LOW-VOLTAGE WIRES—Electrical wires that carry lower voltage, usually 12 volts, than the standard household current, which is 120 volts. Often used for thermostats, doorbells, and outdoor lighting.

TOOLS & MATERIALS YOU NEED

❏ Screwdrivers
❏ Masking tape
❏ Programmable thermostat

DIFFICULTY LEVEL

This project can be completed in a weekend.

1 Start by removing the existing thermostat. Turn off the power to the furnace at the main service panel. Then, remove the thermostat cover.

2 The body of the thermostat is held to a wall plate with screws. Remove these screws and pull the body away from the wall plate. Set the body aside.

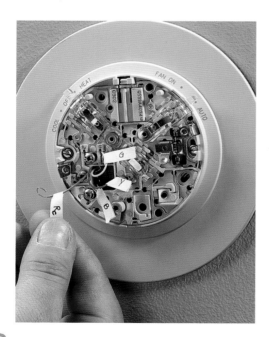

3 The low-voltage wires that power the thermostat are held by screw terminals to the mounting plate. Do not remove the wires until you label them with tape, according to the letter printed on the terminal to which each wire is attached.

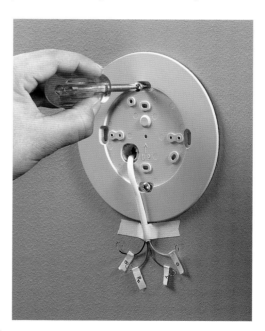

4 Once all the wires are labeled and removed from the mounting plate, tape the cable that holds these wires to the wall to keep it from falling back into the wall. Then unscrew the mounting plate and set it aside (see sidebar, next page).

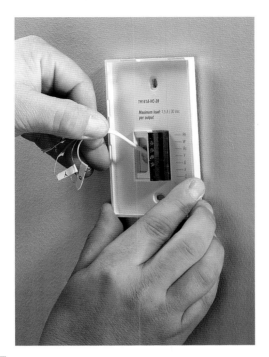

5 Position the new thermostat base on the wall and guide the wires through the central opening. Screw the base to the wall.

6 Check the manufacturer's instructions to establish the correct terminal for each low-voltage wire. Then connect the wires to these terminals, making sure each screw is secure.

7 These thermostats require batteries to store the programs so they won't disappear if the electric power goes out in a storm. Make sure to install these batteries before you snap the thermostat cover in place. Then program the new unit to fit your needs and turn on the power to the furnace.

MERCURY THERMOSTATS

Older model thermostats (and even a few still being made today) often contained one or more small vials of mercury totaling 3 to 4 grams in weight. Because mercury is a highly toxic metal that can cause nerve damage in humans, along with other environmental problems, DO NOT dispose of an old mercury thermometer with your household waste. Instead, bring it to a hazardous waste disposal site, or a mercury recycling site if your area has one (check with your local solid waste disposal agency). The best way to determine if you old thermostat contains mercury is simply to remove the cover and look for the small glass vials or ampules containing the silverfish mercury substance. If you are unsure, it is always better to be safe and keep the device in question out of the normal waste stream.

Repair & Maintenance Projects

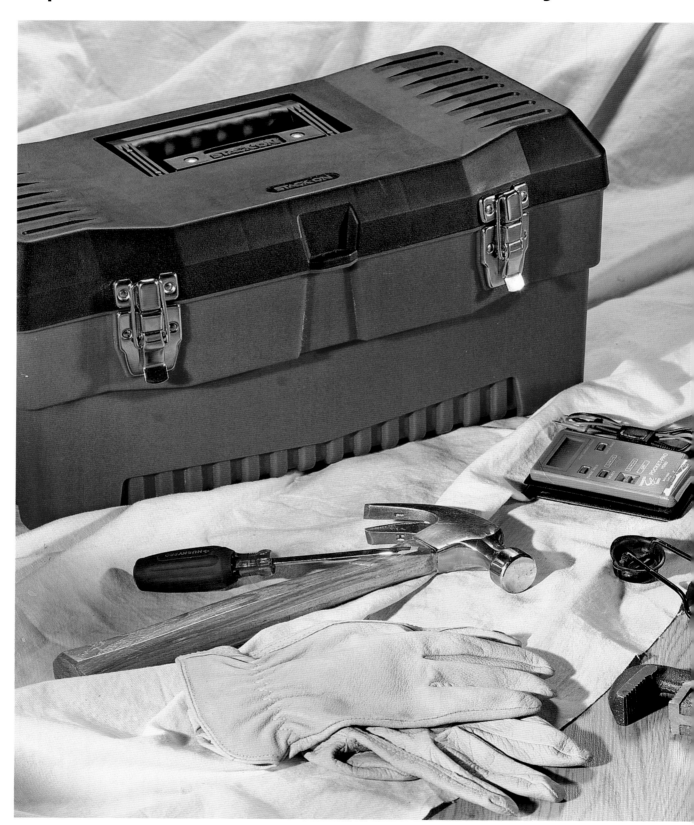

WHICHEVER KIND OF DWELLING YOU LIVE IN, BE IT A SINGLE-FAMILY home, a townhouse, an apartment, or a cabin in the woods, it is a near certainty that your dwelling is populated with major appliances. And even though appliances today, both small and large, are often built to be semi-disposable, you can still prolong their lives and help them operate more efficiently by treating them to regular maintenance and occasional small repairs.

This chapter includes maintenance and repair information for a range of appliances, from ranges to water heaters to washers and dryers. The repair projects are selected because they are among the most common ones you are likely to encounter. But if you follow the maintenance programs described here, you may never need to attempt the repairs.

THIS CHAPTER INCLUDES:

❏ Gas Furnace Tune-up

❏ Maintaining a Refrigerator

❏ Maintaining a Central Air Conditioner

❏ Maintaining a Room Air Conditioner

❏ Maintaining a Gas Water Heater

❏ Maintaining an Electric Water Heater

❏ Electric Range Tune-up

❏ Gas Range Tune-up

❏ Maintaining a Dishwasher

❏ Maintaining a Water Softener

❏ Replacing Dryer Drive Belt

❏ Fixing a Slow-Filling Washing Machine

Gas Furnace Tune-up

ONE OF THE BEST THINGS ABOUT OWNING A GAS FURNACE IS THAT THEY ARE SO POPULAR THAT finding information, parts, and materials to maintain them is relatively easy. Plus, most local gas suppliers employ service technicians who devote all their time to furnace tune-ups and repairs. These technicians are indispensable, especially if you have one of the newer, high-efficiency, condensing furnaces with electronic controls. These are the same kind of things that can make it difficult to work on your family car.

Even if you own the most sophisticated gas furnace on the market, there are still plenty of maintenance tasks you can do yourself to keep the appliance running safely and efficiently. Most of them are not much harder than vacuuming the interior of your car, which is not something you want to pay a high-priced mechanic to do. A few hours spent cleaning and lubricating a gas furnace can improve its efficiency immediately and extend its life in the bargain. Leave the electronic controls and gas valve repairs to experienced technicians, but everything else is fair game.

GAS FURNACE TUNE-UP

GAS SUPPLY CONTROLS

The pilot light, found on older gas furnaces, has a separate gas supply line from the furnace burner. To turn off the pilot for servicing, depress the pilot control knob and twist it to the OFF position. An adjustment screw located next to the pilot light is used to regulate the amount of gas entering the pilot light tube, thereby controlling the flame height.

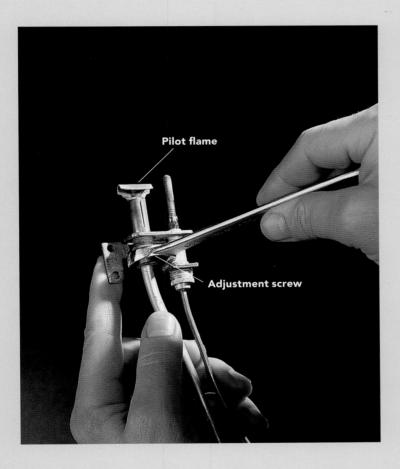

Pilot flame

Adjustment screw

TERMS YOU'LL NEED TO KNOW

FURNACE BURNER—Metal tubes with rectangular slots cut on one side that are attached to the furnace gas control valve with metal tubing. When the thermostat calls for heat, gas is released into these tubs and ignited by a pilot. The burner flames are confined to the combustion chamber in the middle of the furnace.

PILOT BROACH—A specialty tool for cleaning out the pilot orifice on a burner.

JET DRILL—A specialty tool for cleaning out gas jets in a burner.

TOOLS & MATERIALS YOU NEED

- ❏ Screwdrivers
- ❏ Shop vac
- ❏ Nut driver
- ❏ Adjustable wrench
- ❏ Wire brush
- ❏ Pilot broach
- ❏ Jet drill
- ❏ Small stiff-bristle brush or old toothbrush
- ❏ Staple gun and staples
- ❏ New furnace filter
- ❏ Compressed air (from compressor or spray can)
- ❏ Turbine oil
- ❏ Duct tape

DIFFICULTY LEVEL

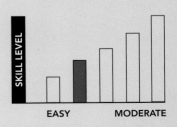

This project can be completed in a weekend.

HOW TO TUNE-UP A GAS FURNACE

1 Turn the electrical switch off. Remove the front door on the furnace cabinet. Sometimes these are held in place with screws. Other models just have a friction fit. To remove this type, lift up the panel, pull out the bottom, and then the top. Set the panel aside. The electricity and gas supply are still on, so don't touch anything but the door. If your furnace has two doors, remove them both but be sure to note which door goes where.

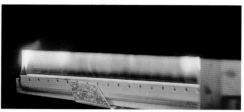

2 Turn the power switch on and look inside the combustion chamber to check the flames rising from the burners. If there is no flame, turn up the thermostat so the burner does come on. If the flames are bright blue with just a little yellow at the tips the burner is pretty clean (top photo). But if the flame is predominantly yellow (bottom photo), the burners need cleaning. Once the flame is inspected, immediately turn off the gas supply and the electrical power to the unit.

3 Clean the combustion compartment using a long nozzle on a shop vac. Dust, rust, and even cobwebs are common debris in furnace cabinets. Lint can also be a big problem if the furnace is located in a laundry room and uses the room air, instead of outside air, as a source of combustion oxygen.

4 Using a screwdriver, loosen any screws on the blower. Use a socket and ratchet to fully remove bolts holding the blower in place. Lift the blower out of the furnace and set it on the floor.

5 Vacuum up any dust, corrosion, and other debris from the blower. Some greasy residue may also be caked onto the fan blades or the motor housing. Remove this build-up with a small brush and a bit of soapy water. Don't soak the motor, and be sure to dry the wet surfaces as soon as they are clean.

6 Remove and dispose of the furnace filter, and then vacuum the filter compartment so it's clean. Buy a new filter that's the same size as the old one, and install it. There are different filters available that go up in price and quality as their filtering capability improves. Buy the best one you can afford and plan to change the filter at least every six months.

7 Clean the pilot by blowing air directly onto the tip. A can of air with a nozzle works well (or, as shown, use a drinking straw to blow air into the exact area). An unclean pilot will cause incorrect readings from the thermocouple.

8 Clean the flame sensor with fine emery cloth or sandpaper, then press the sensor back into its bracket.

(Continued)

9 New furnaces usually have sealed blower shaft bearings that don't need lubrication. But older models have oil fittings on the bearings that are filled with rubber plugs. To lubricate these shafts, just remove the plugs, squirt in a few drops of turbine oil, and replace the plugs. This oil may be available at well-stocked hardware stores, but is a stock item at HVAC dealers.

BLOWER BELT MAINTENANCE

If your blower has a belt, inspect it for cracks or tears. To replace the belt, release the tension on the motor bolt with a wrench, and then completely remove the belt. When you put the new belt on, make sure to adjust the tension so it deflects ¾".

HOT SURFACE IGNITERS

Many furnaces today do not have standing pilot lights and electronic igniters. Instead, hot surface igniters are used. Be sure to gently clean the dust off the igniter, using directed air only.

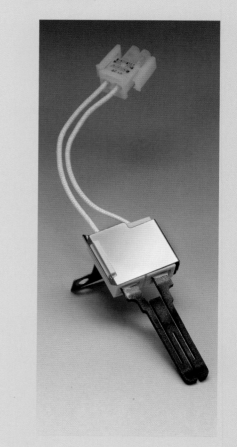

SHUT THE DOOR TIGHTLY

When replacing your furnace door or doors, be sure the doors are installed correctly and shut tight. The door stops on today's furnace doors have an activation switch similar to the one that controls the light inside your refrigerator. If the door is not shut tight, the furnace will not cycle on because of potential danger from fire or carbon monoxide release.

The filters that are used most commonly in gas-fired, forced air furnaces are simple fiberglass batts in card-board or plastic frames. Replacing them couldn't be simpler—you just slide out the old one and slide in the new one. Most furnace manufacturers recommend that this type of filter be replaced monthly or even more frequently during heating or cooling season. But many furnaces employ an alternate style filter that is called either a pleated filter or an accordion filter. These types trap more particles than the simple batt filters and you can go as long as twelve months without replacing them (although every six months is recommended). If your furnace has a pleated filter, you will find it inside a plastic frame located behind a cabinet door next to the furnace burner. You can purchase replacement filters for $20 to $30 at plumbing and heating supply stores, via the Internet, and at some larger home improvement centers.

HOW TO REPLACE A PLEATED FURNACE FILTER

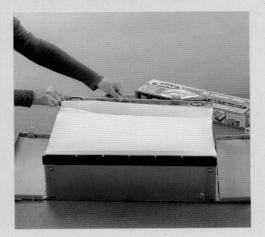

1 With the furnace turned off, remove the filter frame from the housing cabinet. Lift the spacers from the frame and then unsnap the frame latches and collapse the frame sides. Remove and discard the old pleated filter.

2 Fan out the replacement filter and set it inside the filter frame with the cardboard flaps at the edges pointing up. Slip each flap into a channel at the side of the frame.

3 Spread out the pleats so they are evenly spaced and then reinsert the comb-style spacers, beginning in the middle. Make sure each tooth of the spacer separates two pleats and that pleats are not skipped or doubled. This is the only tricky part of the job. Snap the ends of the spacers into the frame side notches. Once you have the middle spacer in place, add the remaining spacers, work-ing from the middle toward the top and bottom. Reassemble the frame and close the latches. Replace the filter frame in your furnace.

Maintaining a Refrigerator

A REFRIGERATOR REMOVES HEAT FROM A BOX AND LEAVES COOLER AIR BEHIND. WHEN A regular maintenance schedule is followed, even an inexpensive model should last at least ten to fifteen years.

The most important refrigerator maintenance job is to make sure that the component that expels the heat (called the condenser coil) works as efficiently as it can. This means keeping it clean. When dust accumulates on the coil, it acts as an insulator, making it harder for the heat to transfer to the surrounding air. As a result, the temperature inside the refrigerator goes up and the only way to bring it down is for the compressor to run more so that refrigerant moves through the system quicker. This wastes energy, exposes the compressor to unnecessary wear, and shortens the life of the appliance (generally, the cost of replacing a failed compressor far exceeds the value of the refrigerator).

Cleaning the condenser coils is a task you should perform at least two or three times a year. Other items on your maintenance checklist should include making sure the door gaskets are in good shape, that the refrigerator is level, and making sure that the condenser drain pan (which collects condensed water that drips off the condenser coils) is empty and clean.

MAINTAIN A REFRIGERATOR

TOOLS & MATERIALS YOU NEED

❏ Vacuum cleaner with a crevice tool
❏ Screwdrivers
❏ Nut drivers
❏ Condenser coil brush

REFRIGERATOR TROUBLESPOT

If you spot water puddling beneath or around your refrigerator, the drain pan for the condenser coils is the first place to check. Whether the coils are located on the back of the fridge, as on the older model appliance below, or underneath, you will find a drain pan that may or may not be removable. Check to see if the drain pan is overflowing (unlikely), out of position, or has a leak.

TERMS YOU'LL NEED TO KNOW

CONDENSER—The part of a refrigeration system where the refrigerant gas is compressed and changed into a liquid, which causes it to give off heat.
EVAPORATOR—The part of a refrigeration system where the refrigerant is a gas that absorbs heat from inside the refrigerator.

DIFFICULTY LEVEL

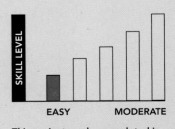

SKILL LEVEL

EASY   MODERATE

This project can be completed in a weekend.

HOW TO CLEAN COILS

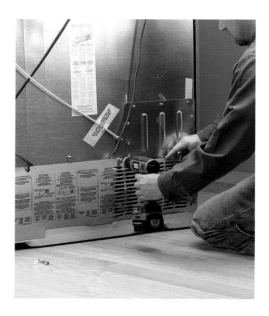

USE A VACUUM CLEANER and crevice tool attachment to clean the coils. This is the best tool for older models with the coils located in a large grid on the back of the appliance. Refrigerators with coils underneath can also be cleaned with a vacuum and crevice attachment, in most cases by removing the toe-kick grill to get access.

IF YOUR COILS ARE LOCATED UNDERNEATH the refrigerator but you have no front panel below the door to get access, you'll need to pull the unit away from the wall and remove the lower access panel to get at the coils with your vacuum cleaner and crevice attachment.

CONDENSER COIL BRUSHES

A faster, more convenient, and much quieter alternative to taking a vacuum cleaner to your condenser coils is to buy a special condenser coil brush. Long handled with bristles shaped to wrap around the coils, these brushes may be purchased at most appliance stores for less than $10. In addition to the coils, the brushes are effective on other parts, like the condenser tubes and fan, that should also be kept dust-free.

CONDENSER DRAIN PAN

Once the coils are clean, pull out the condenser drain pan (both back-mounted and bottom-mounted coil models have this part) and clean it with soapy water. Then dry it and push it back into its slot.

HOW TO REPLACE A GASKET

1 Test your gaskets. The gaskets are the rubber stripping seals that frame the refrigerator and freezer doors. If the gasket seal becomes compromised, energy loss occurs. To check your gaskets, close the doors over a dollar bill and slowly pull it out. There should be some noticeable resistance. If the bill slips out easily, the gasket is worn and should be replaced.

2 The best way to replace a door gasket is to do it progressively at the same time as the old one is being removed. Begin by lifting the rubber flap on the gasket and loosening screws on the top section of the gasket. Pull down on the gasket. If the door is dirty or discolored behind the gasket as it is removed, clean it before installing the new gasket.

3 Slide the new gasket into place and insert the retainer screws so the new gasket fits in exactly the same spot as the old one. If the new gasket is stiff, dip it in warm water to loosen it up. Tighten the retainer screws, taking care not to overtighten and deform the gasket. Once the gasket is in place, test the fit by re-doing the dollar test.

NOTE: Any appliance seller should be able to locate the appropriate gasket based on the make and model number of your appliance. Gaskets range from $50 to $100.

MORE TIPS FOR REFRIGERATOR MAINTENANCE

The refrigerator should be level, especially if it has an icemaker. Put a level on the top of the refrigerator and check, then adjust the roller wheels with a screwdriver. Turning the screws clockwise will lift the corner. Check the level from side-to-side and from front-to-back.

If a door is sagging, it can be adjusted. Loosen the screws at the hinge locations with a screwdriver or a nut driver. Then, lift up the end on the door and retighten the hinges. It may take a couple of tries to get the door adjusted properly. This fix can also solve the problem if the door is not making good contact, as when the freezer door compartments strike the top of the freezer compartment.

Maintaining a Central Air Conditioner

IN MANY WAYS, A CENTRAL AIR CONDITIONER IS JUST A BIG REFRIGERATOR. BOTH UNITS HAVE THE same basic parts, do the same basic thing, and require the same basic maintenance: namely, keeping the condenser coils clean so the heat transfer operates as efficiently as possible.

Unlike refrigerators, central air conditioners are split appliances. The evaporator is inside the house, usually installed in the plenum of a forced air furnace, and the condenser is outdoors, located next to the house. Most of the maintenance work is done outdoors on the condenser.

Cleaning requires removal of all leaves and other debris that may have blown into the unit or between it and the house. It also calls for closely trimming the vegetation next to the unit so it won't reduce free airflow around the condenser cabinet.

MAINTAIN A CENTRAL AIR CONDITIONER

THE SHUTOFF SWITCH

Central air conditioner units must have a disconnect switch mounted on the exterior wall near the unit so you can shut off power to the unit without needing to enter your home.

TOOLS & MATERIALS YOU NEED

- ❏ Screwdrivers
- ❏ Old paintbrush
- ❏ Garden hose
- ❏ Fin comb
- ❏ Level
- ❏ Watering can
- ❏ Lightweight oil
- ❏ Bleach

DIFFICULTY LEVEL

This project can be completed in a weekend.

TERMS YOU'LL NEED TO KNOW

LIGHTWEIGHT OIL—A petroleum-based lubricant, available in liquid or spray form, like 3-In-One oil, that is used for maintenance purposes on light machinery. It is lighter and thinner than SAE 20 motor oil.

HOW TO MAINTAIN A CENTRAL AIR CONDITIONER

1 Before working on the air conditioner, turn off the power to the unit at the service panel or at the disconnect switch mounted near the unit.

2 Remove the screws holding the top grate in place, and lift it off the cabinet. Taking care not to create too much pressure on the electrical harness attached to the fan, loosen the screws and shift the fan mount out of the way. Remove all the leaves and debris from the inside.

3 Direct the nozzle of a garden hose to spray through the housing and drive debris out from the fins. Set the nozzle for a spray pattern that is gentle enough it won't cause damage but has enough pressure to dislodge dirt and debris.

4 Carefully brush any dirt and dust from between the condenser coil fins using a soft-bristle, 2" paint brush. Then, using a shop vac, clean the dust from areas that the brush can't reach.

5 Straighten any evaporator fins that are bent with a fin comb. Work carefully because the fins are easy to damage. Fin combs function in much the same way as hair combs, but unlike hair, fins can't grow back if they're damaged, so be gentle and don't do any unnecessary combing.

6 If the fan motor has oil ports (usually covered with small black rubber plugs), remove the plugs and squeeze four or five drops of lightweight oil into each port. Replace the rubber plugs.

7 Check the outside housing cabinet for level by placing a level on top. Make sure the level is resting evenly on multiple points. Central air main unit cabinet tops are seldom flat. Shim it with strips of galvanized or aluminum flashing or with galvanized washers if it is not level. A level air conditioner works more efficiently and runs more quietly than an out-of-level one.

8 The evaporator unit inside the furnace has a drain pan to collect condensate and direct it to a drain. This drain can clog with bacteria. To free it, mix a couple of tablespoons of bleach in a cup of hot water. Then remove the end of the drain hose and pour the bleach solution into it.

Maintaining a Room Air Conditioner

ROOM AIR CONDITIONERS ARE CLEVER, HIGHLY USEFUL DEVICES. AS MOST PEOPLE KNOW, AIR conditioners are driven by compressors that can make quite a bit of noise. But few people realize how loud an air conditioner would be if the designers didn't locate the compressor on the exterior side. To verify this, stand 5 feet away from an air conditioner on the inside of the house and listen to the noise. Then go outside and stand 10 feet away from the same unit. It's much louder outside because that's where the compressor is located.

Because so much of a room air conditioner is located outside the house, the appliance gets a lot of exposure to the elements, so you should give it a yearly clean up to keep it working well. Also keep in mind that you can leave an air conditioner in the window all year long, or take it out after the cooling season. The units are designed to tolerate either approach. But if you do leave it in, cover it with a hood or simple plastic sheeting during the winter. If you live in a very cold climate, taking the unit out of the window for the winter is a good idea. Not only does removing it protect it from damage, it helps you save heating dollars and it improves the winter view and allows more passive solar heat into the house.

MAINTAIN A ROOM AIR CONDITIONER

ACCESS PANELS

Room air conditioners have a removable front panel that usually contains the filter. The panel is held against the appliance body with screws or clips that need to be removed to get the panel off. On many room air conditioners, the filter can be pulled out of a slot in the front panel without removing the panel from the unit. This is helpful, since the filter should be washed and dried once a month at a minimum.

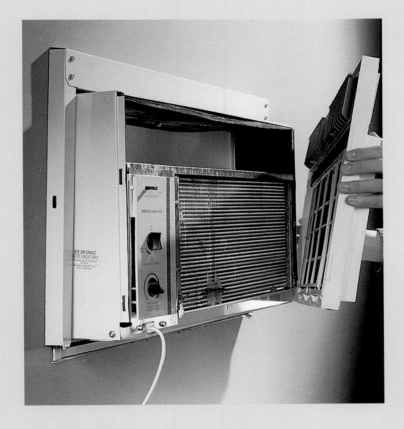

TERMS YOU'LL NEED TO KNOW

EVAPORATOR FINS—Soft aluminum fins that are attached to the evaporator tubing; they pull heat from the room and transfer it to the refrigerant.

TOOLS & MATERIALS YOU NEED

- ❑ Screwdrivers
- ❑ Nut drivers
- ❑ Vacuum with a crevice tool
- ❑ Plastic container and paintbrush
- ❑ Garden hose and nozzle
- ❑ Evaporator fin comb
- ❑ Room air conditioner cover hood of plastic sheeting

DIFFICULTY LEVEL

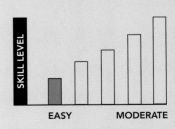

This project can be completed in a weekend.

HOW TO MAINTAIN A ROOM AIR CONDITIONER

1 To remove a room air conditioner, first unplug the power cord, then loosen the side panels, lift up the window sash and pull the air conditioner into the room. It is always a good idea to have a helper on the outdoors side to make sure the appliance doesn't fall out the wrong way.

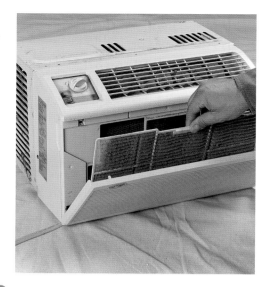

2 Remove the filter (they usually slide out of the top or side when you pull on the plastic filter frame tab) and clean it with soap and water. Rinse it thoroughly with clean water and let it dry. If the filter is damaged, buy a new one from your unit's manufacturer, or buy a universal type that can be cut to fit any air conditioner.

3 Remove the air conditioner outer cabinet housing by unscrewing the screws that hold it in place. Thoroughly wash the inside and outside of the cabinet and set it aside.

4 Use a vacuum cleaner (preferably a wet-and-dry shop vac) with a crevice tool to remove the dust and debris from inside the air conditioner unit.

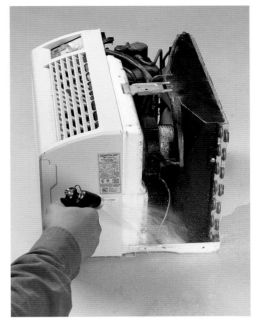

5 Once all the debris is removed, wash the inside surfaces and non-electrical parts with warm soapy water, applied with an old paintbrush. Protect any electrical components with plastic to keep them from getting wet.

6 Once the unit is clean, rinse it with a garden hose and let it dry. Then, remove the plastic that's covering the electrical components and let the unit dry for at least a day.

7 Before reassembly, check that the evaporator fins are straight and parallel to the other fins. If they aren't, they will not work efficiently. Use an inexpensive fin comb to straighten them. These tools are available at hardware stores and heating, ventilation, and air-conditioning suppliers.

8 If you have the storage capacity, remove the air conditioner for the winter, clean it up, and put it away. If not, leave it in the window and cover it with an insulated hood or plastic sheeting. Also, make sure to close the vents to reduce the amount of cold air that will pass through the unit into the house.

Maintaining a Gas Water Heater

A GAS WATER HEATER MAY BE MORE COMPLICATED THAN AN ELECTRIC MODEL, AND IT CERTAINLY costs more and is harder to install. But it's much cheaper to run. In many areas, the cost of running an electric water heater is 60% more than natural gas. The cost is the good news. The maintenance is the not- so-good news. But it's not really bad news, either. There are just a few things to take care of and most of these apply to an electric heater as much as they do to a gas model. Here's a checklist:

- Make sure the T&P (temperature and pressure) relief valve is working properly.
- Check the tank drain valve for leaks. If it does leak, replace it.
- Check the sacrificial anode rod and replace it if it is severely corroded.
- Make sure the flue is working properly.
- Clean the burner assembly and replace the thermocouple.

If you have the parts on hand and a few basic tools, this whole tune-up should not take more than three or four hours.

MAINTAIN A GAS WATER HEATER

THE PRESSURE RELIEF VALVE

Test the operation of the pressure relief valve (sometimes called a T & P valve) at least once a year. It is usually attached to a copper drain pipe with an open end and is located near the top of the tank. Lift up the valve test lever and release it. The lever should snap back and allow a quick burst of hot water out of the tank. If the lever is stuck or it moves but doesn't release the hot water, replace the valve. To do this job, first turn off the water and the gas to the heater. Let the water cool, then remove the old valve using a pipe wrench turned counterclockwise. Cover the threads of a new valve with Teflon tape and thread it into the valve hole (top photo). Tighten it with a pipe wrench. Then, twist the drain pipe into the female opening of the valve, making sure the drain pipe is vertical (bottom photo).

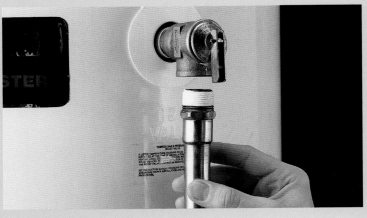

TERMS YOU'LL NEED TO KNOW

THERMOCOUPLE—A device, consisting of two dissimilar metals, that is wired into an electrical circuit. When heated, the metals create a small electrical current.

TOOLS & MATERIALS YOU NEED

- ❑ Channel-type pliers
- ❑ Socket wrench
- ❑ Pipe wrench
- ❑ Adjustable wrench
- ❑ Wire
- ❑ Shop vac
- ❑ Teflon tape
- ❑ T&P valve
- ❑ Water heater drain valve
- ❑ Anode rod
- ❑ Candle or incense stick

DIFFICULTY LEVEL

SKILL LEVEL

EASY   MODERATE

This project can be completed in a few hours.

1 Water heater manufacturers line steel water tanks with glass to prevent the tanks from corroding. But some pinholes always occur and these can rust. To prevent this, anode tubes are installed in the tanks. These rods corrode at a faster rate than the iron in the steel tank. And, as they corrode, they shed electrons that coat the inside of the tank and fill the pinholes, thus preventing rust. To inspect the anode rod, unthread the rod with a socket wrench and withdraw it. If it is degraded, it should be replaced.

2 Purchase a replacement anode tube and slide it into the opening. Coat the threaded end with Teflon tape or pipe joint compound, and tighten it in place with a socket wrench.

WHAT IF:

If the tank drain valve is leaking, it probably needs replacing. Turn off the water and gas supply to the tank. Then hook a garden hose to the valve and run it to a floor drain, laundry sink, or outdoors. Once the tank is empty, turn on the water for a minute to loosen up some of the sediment at the bottom of the tank. Let this water drain out, then turn off the water, remove the hose, and unthread the valve using channel-type pliers or a pipe wrench. Coat the threads of a new valve with Teflon tape and thread valve into the tank.

TIP: To check if the flue is working properly, wait until the burner comes on, and then hold a smoking candle or piece of incense next to the flue hat. Because the heater creates a draft when the burner is running, the smoke from the candle or incense should be drawn up into the flue. If it isn't, call a service technician right away for a professional inspection and repair.

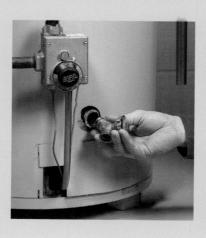

1 A thermocouple keeps the gas valve open so that gas flows to the burner when the thermostat calls for it. If the burner doesn't light when there's no hot water in the tank, this usually means that the thermocouple should be replaced. It's a good idea to clean the burner when you replace the thermocouple. To do these jobs, first remove the burner assembly by loosening the nuts that hold it in place. Then pull out the burner.

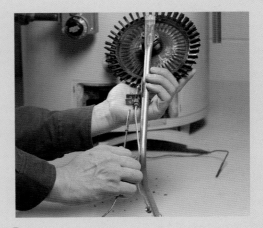

2 Very gently, tap the edge of the burner on the floor to loosen any scale, then remove the scale with a wire brush. Clean the burner jets with a piece of wire, and then vacuum the jets and the bottom of the tank with a shop vac.

3 Install the new thermocouple following the manufacturer's directions. Then, coil any excess thermocouple wire out of the way and reinstall the burner. Make sure all the connections are tight. Reinstall the cover plate, fill the tank with water, and turn on the gas.

Maintaining an Electric Water Heater

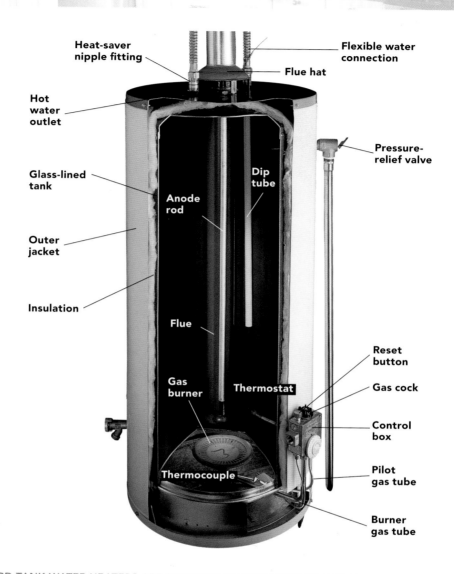

Heat-saver nipple fitting

Flexible water connection

Flue hat

Hot water outlet

Pressure-relief valve

Glass-lined tank

Dip tube

Anode rod

Outer jacket

Insulation

Flue

Reset button

Gas burner

Thermostat

Gas cock

Control box

Pilot gas tube

Thermocouple

Burner gas tube

STANDARD TANK WATER HEATERS ARE DESIGNED SO THAT REPAIRS ARE SIMPLE. ALL WATER HEATERS have convenient access panels that make it easy to replace worn-out parts. When buying new water heater parts, make sure the replacements match the specifications of your water heater. Most water heaters have a nameplate that lists the information needed, including the pressure rating of the tank and the voltage and wattage ratings of the electric heating elements.

Many water heater problems can be avoided with routine yearly maintenance. Water heaters last about ten years on average, but with regular maintenance, a water heater can last twenty years or more.

The pressure-relief valve is an important safety device that should be checked at least once each year and replaced, if needed. When replacing the pressure-relief valve, shut off the water and drain several gallons of water from the tank.

MAINTAIN AN ELECTRIC WATER HEATER

TOOLS & MATERIALS YOU NEED

- ❏ Screwdriver
- ❏ Gloves
- ❏ Neon circuit tester
- ❏ Channel-type pliers
- ❏ Masking tape
- ❏ Replacement heating element or thermostat
- ❏ Replacement gasket
- ❏ Pipe joint compound

TIPS FOR MAINTAINING A WATER HEATER

Flush the water heater once a year by draining several gallons of water from the tank. Flushing removes sediment buildup that causes corrosion and reduces heating efficiency.

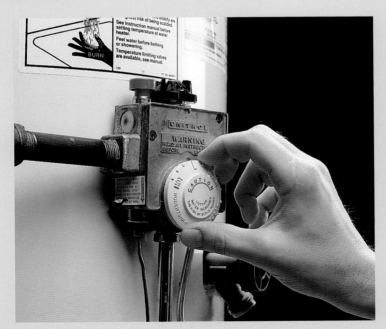

Lower the temperature setting on thermostat to 120° F. Lower temperature setting reduces damage to tank caused by overheating and also reduces energy use.

DIFFICULTY LEVEL

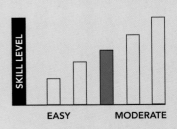

SKILL LEVEL

EASY   MODERATE

This project can be completed in a weekend.

HOW TO REPLACE AN ELECTRIC THERMOSTAT

 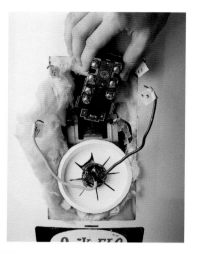 

1 Turn off power at main service panel. Remove access panel on side of heater, and test for current.

2 Disconnect thermostat wires, and label connections with masking tape. Pull old thermostat out of mounting clips. Snap new thermostat into place, and reconnect wires.

3 Press thermostat reset button, then use a screwdriver to set thermostat to desired temperature. Replace insulation and access panel. Turn on power.

HOW TO REPLACE AN ELECTRIC HEATING ELEMENT

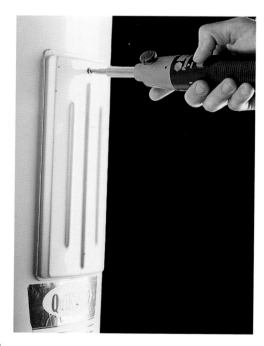 

1 Remove access panel on side of water heater. Shut off power to water heater. Close the shutoff valves, then drain the tank.

2 Wearing protective gloves, carefully move insulation aside. CAUTION: Test for current, then disconnect wires on heating element. Remove protective collar.

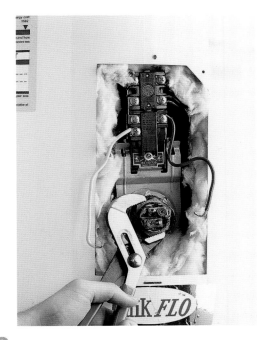

3 Unscrew the heating element with channel-type pliers. Remove old gasket from around water heater opening. Coat both sides of new gasket with pipe joint compound.

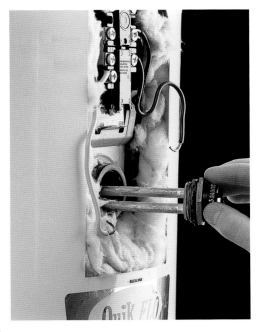

4 Slide new gasket over heating element and screw element into the tank. Tighten element with channel-type pliers.

5 Replace protective collar and reconnect all wires. Turn on hot water faucets throughout house, then turn on water heater shutoff valves. When tap water runs steadily, close faucets.

6 Use a screwdriver to set thermostat to desired temperature. Press thermostat reset buttons. Fold insulation over thermostat, and replace the access panel. Turn on power.

Electric Range Tune-up

COMPARED TO A GAS RANGE, A TRADITIONAL ELECTRIC RANGE IS EXCEEDINGLY SIMPLE. Basically, it consists of a box oven, heated by a large electric resistance coil on the bottom and a large broiling coil on the top. Outside the box, there's a cooktop surface that usually features four electric resistance heating elements. These elements are often grouped in pairs with different wattage ratings, typically from 1000 to 2500 watts.

The beauty of an electric range is threefold: it's compact, easy to install, and can successfully cook just about anything you want. It never gives off obnoxious gas fumes, it does not have pilot lights that wash out when water is spilled on them, and it has no open flames exposed that can ignite potholders or neckties.

Some cooks contend that electric ranges don't heat up as quickly as gas models. But some comparison tests have proved this to be wrong. What may differentiate these two appliances is control. Adjusting the height of a visible flame is a purely analog experience. Adjusting a knob to a number isn't the same thing.

ELECTRIC RANGE TUNE-UP

THE RIGHT RECEPTACLE

An electric range requires a very specific type of receptacle. If your range works but the clock, timer, and oven light don't, the chances are that your appliance is not plugged into the right type of outlet. Electric range receptacles have two current sources: they provide 240-volt power for the heating elements and separate 120-volt power for the accessories. A typical range receptacle is rated for 50 amps.

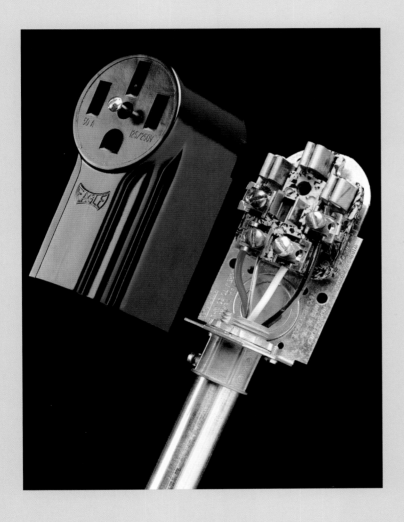

TERMS YOU'LL NEED TO KNOW

MULTIMETER—A battery-operated testing device that measures voltage, resistance (ohms), continuity, and grounding. Autoranging models require less set-up than manual models. Also called a Volt-Ohm meter.

DIFFICULTY LEVEL

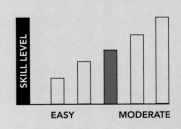

SKILL LEVEL

EASY   MODERATE

This project can be completed in a day.

HOW TO TUNE-UP AN ELECTRIC RANGE

1 Begin by turning off the power to the range at the main service panel. Then lift up the range top and support it on its side braces. Some models have a single support brace that is hinged on one side of the cabinet.

2 If an oven light doesn't work, but the bulb is okay, then the socket must be damaged. To replace it, first remove the bulb cover from inside the oven, then go to the back of the appliance and depress the side clips on the socket and push it into the oven cavity. Pull it out completely by grasping the bulb.

3 Insert the replacement socket, with bulb installed, into the opening inside the oven box so it clicks into place. Test the new bulb and socket.

4 If a burner heating element isn't working (the burner should glow uniformly as it heats up), remove it from its socket by pulling it straight out.

5 Test the element for resistance with an autoranging multimeter. If the meter shows partial resistance, usually 10 to 70 ohms, the element is okay. If it shows no resistance or infinite resistance, the element must be replaced.

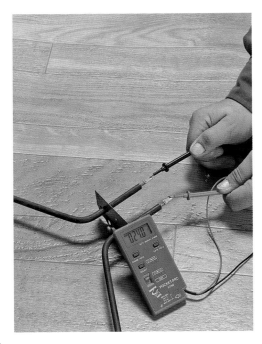

7 Touch each end of the element with a multimeter probe. The meter should find some resistance, usually 20 to 40 ohms. If none registers, the element should be replaced.

6 The heating and broiling elements inside the oven are held in place with screws driven through mounting brackets. If either of these heater coils doesn't work, remove it to check it for resistance as you checked the burner element.

MULTIMETER

One very useful tool for fixing appliances is an inexpensive electrical diagnostic device known as a multimeter or Volt-Ohm meter. It is a simple battery powered device that allows you to do a variety of tests on small and large appliances, as well as the wiring in the house itself. But for fledgling repair people, it is suggested that you confine the use of the tool to measuring whether the appliance, which won't run, has continuity or resistance in the wires. Continuity exists if electrical current can flow from point A to point B. If the flow of current is blocked or broken, as when a fuse blows or a circuit breaker trips, then the appliance being tested does not have continuity.

Using the multimeter is simple. It has two metal probes: one on the end of a red wire and the other on the end of a black wire. First, you use knobs or buttons to set the device to the test for continuity (see your owner's manual). Then, touch one probe to each side of the part (such as a switch) being tested and read the display screen.

Gas Range Tune-up

GAS RANGES AND OVENS HAVE CHANGED DRAMATICALLY OVER THE PAST GENERATION. Long-gone are the days of igniting an oven with a long kitchen match or constantly lighting and relighting a stubborn pilot light that won't stay lit. Today, gas ranges are made with electronic ignition, which eliminates the need for a pilot light. When you turn the burner or oven to the "Light" setting, you hear a clicking noise that is an electrode firing electronic sparks that ignite the gas. It is a much safer system that requires far less maintenance than the old standing pilot light gas ranges.

From time to time, especially if you have a major spillover, the gas burners will require some cleaning. Dirty burners are easy to remove, disassemble, and clean. In fact, on modern sealed burners there is only one gas port, not a whole ring of small ones that clog easily, as in the old days.

Working on a gas range requires a couple of common sense precautions. First, always turn off the gas supply to the range and pull the power cord before doing any work. Second, if you smell a strong gas odor, immediately turn off the gas supply at the meter, exit the building, and call the gas company hotline with a cell phone or a neighbor's phone.

GAS RANGE TUNE-UP

TOOLS & MATERIALS YOU NEED

- ❏ Screwdrivers
- ❏ Sewing needle
- ❏ Old toothbrush
- ❏ Scrubbing pad
- ❏ Flashlight

BEWARE: STEEL WOOL ON BURNERS

Some people use steel wool to clean burners. If the stove has electronic ignition, this is a mistake. The steel wool can leave bits and pieces of steel that short out the electrode that lights the burner. To avoid this problem and still clean well, use either an abrasive pad such as the Scotch brand pad or a plastic mesh.

THE GAS HOOK-UP

Gas is supplied to your gas range through a flexible supply line that is connected to a shutoff valve on the gas supply pipe. The supply pipe shutoff typically comes up through the floor in the range installation area. Making this connection can be tricky and dangerous. It is not uncommon for inexperienced installers to disrupt the connection while pushing the appliance into the installation area after the hookup. Unless you have a lot of experience with gas pipes, have a pro do this job for you. In some areas, homeowners may not work on their gas pipes under any circumstances.

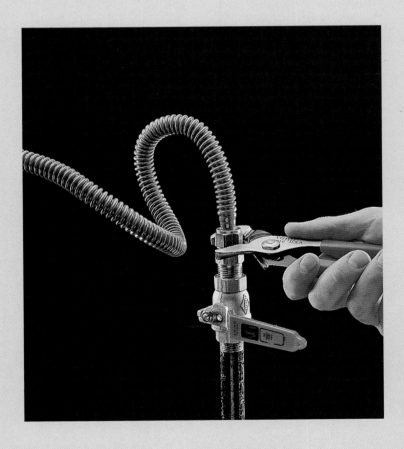

DIFFICULTY LEVEL

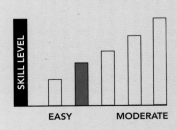

SKILL LEVEL

EASY   MODERATE

This project can be completed in a weekend.

HOW TO CLEAN GAS BURNERS

1 Sealed gas burners are designed to be disassembled easily. If you've been using the range, wait until it has had plenty of time to cool, and then lift off the grate of the underperforming burner. Remove the cast-iron burner cap to expose the burner head.

2 Clean the electrode with a nonmetal, abrasive pad and hot soapy water. NOTE: If you can hear good gas flow when you turn the burner to light but the gas won't ignite, a dirty electrode is a likely culprit.

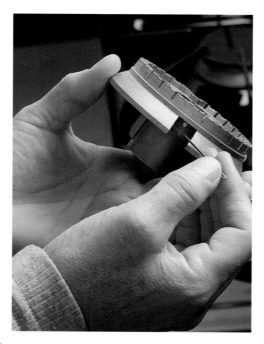

3 Remove the burner head and clear the gas port (there is only one) with a sewing needle. A partially clogged port is usually the reason for diminished flame strength.

4 If the burner grates and burner caps have stubborn build-ups or discolorations, soak them in hot soapy water for 20 to 30 minutes. Then, clean them with a scrub pad. Scrub out the narrow slits in the crown of the burner head with an old toothbrush.

Oven temperatures are hard to control and can often vary by 20° or more. If your bake times are consistently fast or slow, your controls may need recalibrating. Gas ovens have a thermostat, often located on the back of the control knob. To make an adjustment, remove the temperature setting, loosen the setscrews, and adjust the screw position. Use an oven thermometer to test the temperature.

If your gas stovetop burners fire up fine but your oven won't light, check the gas shutoff valve inside the stove box. In most cases, you'll need to remove the lower broiler door or the drawer front to get at the shutoff valve. Once you locate this valve, check to see if it is in the "open" or "closed" position. It should be open.

Oven doors are often sealed with a heat-proof gasket. If the seal is not tight, remove the door by opening it partway and lifting straight upward. Clean the door, the gasket, and the strike points where the door and oven meet. Do not use a chemical oven cleaner on or near the gasket. Hot soapy water and a mild scrubbing pad are best. (If you have a self-cleaning oven, do not clean the inside of any glass in the oven door).

Gas ranges have air intake vents to supply fresh air to the gas burners. Without the correct amount of oxygen, burners will not operate properly. The vents may be located just about anywhere. Try the back edge of the cooktop or underneath the broiler (or pot storage) door. Your owner's manual should identify this location. Once you have located the vents, check for blockages. Remove any blockages and clean the vents.

Maintaining a Dishwasher

DISHWASHERS ARE DURABLE, LOW-MAINTENANCE APPLIANCES. THE FEW PROBLEMS THAT DO occur can be solved relatively easily. Replace a defective door gasket to eliminate leaks. If the gasket appears to be in good condition, adjust the door catch: loosen the retaining screws on the door catch, reposition it, and tighten the screws.

Replace a damaged or kinked drain hose to allow the unit to drain properly. Relocate water or waste lines that rest against the dishwasher to reduce excessive noise levels.

Clogged water lines can present more serious problems. A clogged screen or defective solenoid can keep the dishwasher from filling correctly. You can clean the inlet valve, which may solve the problem, but solenoid repair requires professional attention.

MAINTAIN A DISHWASHER

A standard dishwasher is a slide-in appliance that can be pulled out from the cabinet when repairs are necessary.

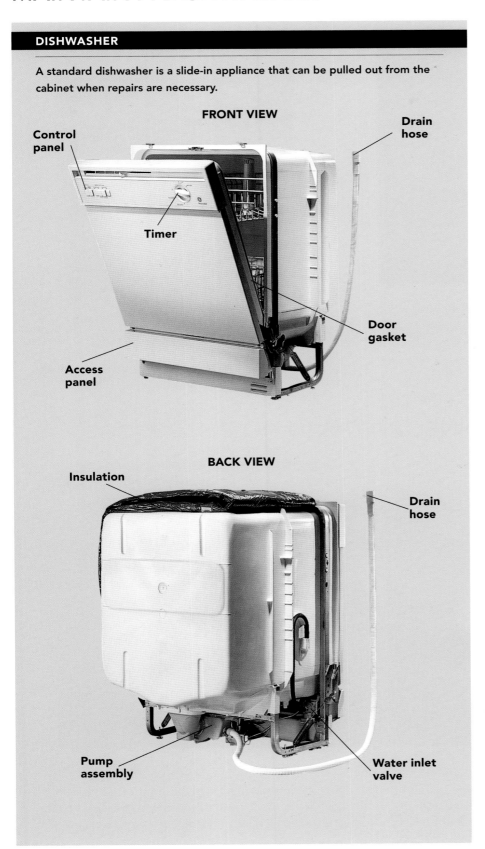

FRONT VIEW

Control panel

Timer

Access panel

Drain hose

Door gasket

BACK VIEW

Insulation

Drain hose

Pump assembly

Water inlet valve

DIFFICULTY LEVEL

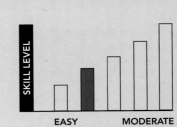

SKILL LEVEL

EASY   MODERATE

This project can be completed in a weekend.

TIPS FOR DISHWASHER MAINTENANCE

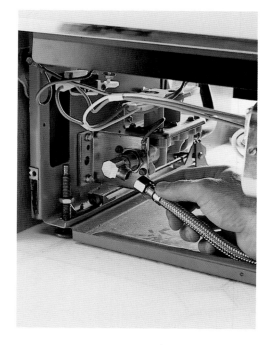

INSTALL AN AIR GAP to make your drain system work more effectively with less chance of backing up. The air gap fitting mounts in your sink deck and has one hose that comes from the dishwasher and another that leads to the sink drain, usually through the garbage disposer.

FOR MAXIMUM SECURITY, replace your water supply lines with burst-proof braided supply tubes.

HOW TO DISCONNECT A DRAIN HOSE

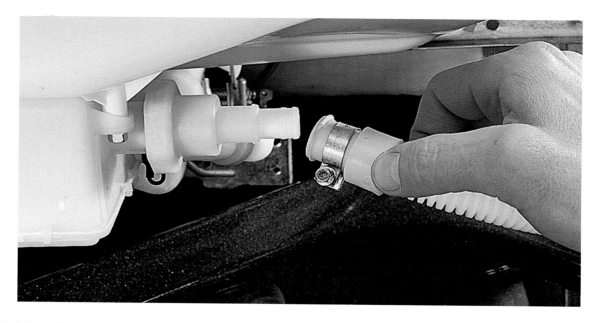

TO TURN OFF POWER AND WATER SUPPLY, remove the lower panel of the unit (held in place by clips or screws). Place a baking pan or bowl under the pump to catch any water trapped in the drain hose. Loosen the hose clamp with pliers or a screwdriver. Remove hose from pump. Detach the other end of the hose from drain or garbage disposer beneath sink. Clean hose with water and bleach, or replace. Restore power and water supply. Test unit to make sure it drains properly.

HOW TO REPLACE A DOOR GASKET

INSPECT THE GASKET AROUND THE DOOR. If it is cracked or damaged, replace it with a new one. Disconnect the electrical power at the main service panel. Pull out the bottom dish rack. Remove the old gasket, using a screwdriver to pry up the tabs or loosen the retaining screws that hold it in place. Soak the new gasket in warm soapy water to make it more pliable and to lubricate it. Install the new gasket by pressing or sliding it into its track. If the gasket has screws or clips, refasten as you go. Work from the center of the door to the ends.

HOW TO TEST A VALVE & REPLACE THE VALVE SCREEN

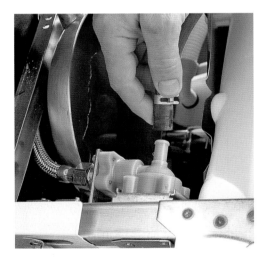

1 Turn off the power and water supply. Remove the access panel and locate the water supply connection. Disconnect wires from the inlet valve terminals. Attach continuity tester clip to one terminal and touch the probe to the other. If the tester does not glow, the solenoid is faulty and should be replaced. To replace the screen, place a shallow pan beneath the valve. Release the clamp and pull the fill tube from the valve outlet.

2 Disconnect the water supply tube. Loosen the valve bracket screws and remove valve. Remove the screen, using a small screwdriver. Replace the screen with a new one and reinstall the valve.

Maintaining a Water Softener

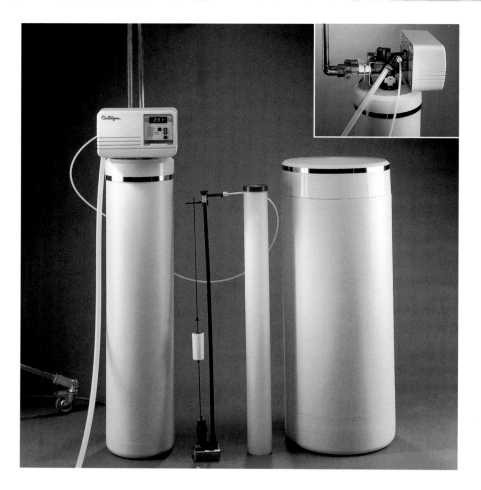

A WATER SOFTENER LOWERS THE CONTENT OF "HARD" MINERALS IN WATER—MAGNESIUM AND calcium—and replaces them with sodium or potassium to help prolong the life of pipes and appliances. It has just a few mechanical parts—valves to control water flow in and out of the tank, and a timer, which regulates the recharging of the mineral tank by the brine tank.

If your water becomes hard, the brine tank may just need additional salt or potassium pellets. Because household demands vary, check your supply every week to determine how often the salt or potassium supply should be replenished (typically every couple of months).

An improperly set timer can cause hard water. Adjust it to run more frequently to ensure a constant supply of soft water. Iron content also causes hard water. Measure the iron content of your water supply occasionally, or add a water filter to help reduce the iron flow into the water softener.

Repair problems generally arise in the brine line or the control unit. Inspect the brine line every two years for buildup of sediment from the water supply or foreign particles in the salt or potassium. If the control unit needs servicing, remove it and bring it to your nearest dealer. Follow the removal instructions in the owner's manual for your particular unit.

HOW TO INSPECT & CLEAN BRINE CONNECTIONS

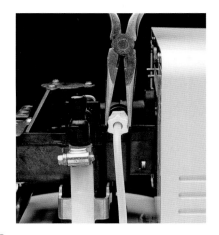

1 Unplug softener. Divert the water supply by turning the bypass valve, or closing the inlet valve and turning on the nearest faucet. Turn timer dial to backwash. With a needlenose pliers, remove the compression nut connecting the brine line to the control unit. Inspect line for obstructions.

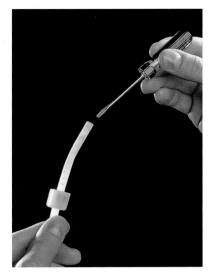

2 Remove particles or residue from the line, using a small screwdriver. Flush line with warm water—a funnel or kitchen baster is useful for this task—then reattach the brine line.

3 Inspect the brine injector. Do not reconnect power or make any changes to the supply or control dial. To gain access to the brine injector, which is often directly below the brine line connection, use a screwdriver to remove the cover. Unscrew injector from housing.

4 Pull off the injector filter screen covering the injector. Wash it with soap and water. Blow into injector or wipe it out with a soft cloth to clean. Do not use a sharp object that might scratch the metal and damage the injector. Reattach screen and screw injector back into place. Attach the cover. Return bypass valve to original position, or open inlet valve and turn off faucet. Reset the control dial and plug in softener.

DIFFICULTY LEVEL

SKILL LEVEL

EASY   MODERATE

This project can be completed in a weekend.

Replacing a Dryer Drive Belt

THE SIMPLEST CLOTHES DRYERS ARE THE ELECTRIC MODELS BECAUSE THEIR HEATING ELEMENTS are resistance units not that much different than the ones that make your toast. Gas models are somewhat more complicated, but they are still card-carrying members of the tried-and-true technology world. Both types are very reliable, which is not to say that they never break down.

When a clothes dryer breaks down, one of the most common problems is a broken drive belt. The symptoms are a loud banging noise, followed by a drum that stops turning. For such a big problem, the solution is pretty simple. The hardest part is gaining access to the drum inside the dryer cabinet. While all brands are different, the process is nearly the same. If you don't run into any trouble and have the replacement part on hand, the job should take about two hours.

REPLACE A DRYER DRIVE BELT

TOOLS & MATERIALS YOU NEED

- ❑ 1½"-wide putty knife
- ❑ Flathead screwdriver
- ❑ Scrap wood blocks
- ❑ Replacement drive belt for your dryer

PREVENTING DRYER FIRES

The U.S. Consumer Products Safety Commission estimates that clothes dryers are associated with more than 15,000 fires each year that result in property damage, injury, and in the worst cases, death. Dryers rank third among the appliances in our homes that start fires, with only stoves and fixed heating systems ranking higher.

Any household electrical appliance, including dryers, require periodic inspection to ensure they are working properly. It is suggested you (or a professional) inspect and replace worn parts and clean its interior to prevent the build up of lint and other fibers that can cause a malfunction. To protect your home and family, make sure you operate your dryer with these precautions in mind:

• Never leave the house while your dryer is running—a malfunction can occur at anytime, often with serious consequences. If the dryer does malfunction, immediately turn it off and disconnect the power cord. Repair it immediately.

• Make sure your dryer is vented to an outside wall and check to see that its exhaust vent is unobstructed and its outdoor vent flap opens frequently. If air is not being directed through the duct, there may be a blockage. In order to remove the blockage from the exhaust path, you may have to disconnect the exhaust duct from the dryer. Be sure to reconnect the vent and the duct before restarting the dryer.

• Keep the area in which your dryer is located free from clutter. Make sure there are no combustible materials such as boxes or clothing near the dryer. Use caution when drying clothing saturated in hazardous chemicals by washing them thoroughly. Then use the lowest heat setting and do not allow contaminated clothing to sit in the dryer or basket with other clothes.

• Remove the lint filter, thoroughly clean it after each use, and reinstall it. Never operate the dryer without the filter. Doing so can cause lint, threads, fibers, and dust to get entrapped in its internal mechanical parts where they can combust or cause other problems.

DIFFICULTY LEVEL

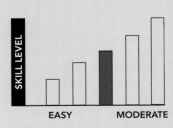

This project can be completed in a few hours.

1 Start by turning off the power to the dryer at the service panel. Then slip a putty knife blade between the cabinet top and front, and push. This should release the hold down clip. Do the same at the other corner, then lift up the top and lean it against the wall. Some top panels are also attached with screws located on the bottom of the lint trap located next to the control panel.

2 Move to the lower front panel and slide the knife, or a flat screwdriver blade, between the panel and the side of the dryer cabinet. Twist the tool to release the hold down clip. Then do the same to the other side. Lift off the panel.

3 Once the lower panel is off, temporarily support the drum with a couple blocks of scrap wood. This will keep the drum from falling when the front panel is removed.

4 The bottom of the front panel is attached to both sides with screws. Loosen these so the panel is free but don't remove the screws.

5 The top of the front panel is attached to both sides with screws located on the inside just below the top lip. Remove these screws.

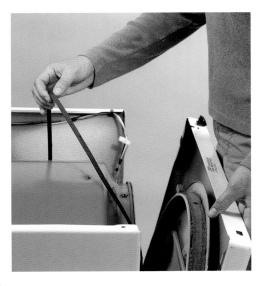

6 Tip the top of the front panel away from the cabinet and support it with your leg. Then pull out the old drive belt, throw it away, and slide the new belt over the drum. Carefully press the front panel back in place and tighten the screws. Remove the wood support blocks so the bottom of the belt can slide back into the cabinet.

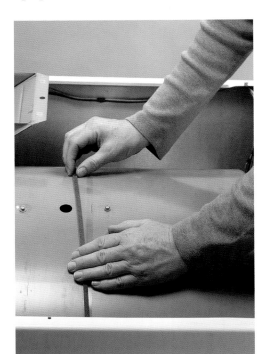

7 Slip the new belt into the same groove that the old belt occupied. If the belt has one grooved side, place it down against the drum.

Idler pulley

8 Loop the drive belt around the motor pulley by pushing the idler pulley toward the motor to create enough clearance. Once the belt is attached to the motor, release the idler and turn the drum counterclockwise several times to make sure the belt is engaged properly.

Fixing a Slow-filling Washing Machine

CLOTHES WASHERS ARE VERY RELIABLE APPLIANCES. STORIES ABOUND OF MACHINES THAT RUN for 20, 30, or even 40 years without any problems at all. This is good, because when they do break down, major repairs are usually so complicated that they're best left to a professional. Unlike clothes dryers, which are largely the same machines no matter who builds them, washers have a great deal of variation among manufacturers. Differences can be in the type of agitator used, where the door is located, how much water and power they consume, or one of many other variables. These differences are reflected in the problems your specific machine might develop and in how it is repaired.

One problem that is shared by all washers is a slow-filling tub. And this is almost always the result of blockages in the inlet screens that are installed to block sediment from getting into the machine and damaging the components. These screens are located in the inlet ports on the back of the washer. To gain access to them, you have to remove the fill hoses.

Usually, these hoses are made of neoprene or some other plastic substitute for rubber. While these hoses are reliable, a failure can send thousands of gallons of water into your house. If you're gone for the day, a lot of water can accumulate in your basement by the time you get home. Because of this, braided metal hoses were developed to eliminate the danger of bursting. So, when you're cleaning the inlet screens, replace the hoses.

FIX A SLOW-FILLING WASHING MACHINE

WHAT ABOUT SLOW DRAINING?

A slow-filling washing machine is easy to detect, but problems in the drain system can be trickier to diagnose. If your clothes are taking too long to dry, it may mean that the washing machine is not draining properly and the clothes are just too wet when you remove them. One way to test drain speed is to set the cycle timer to final spin with the washing machine tub full. Shut the lid and let the final spin cycle start and run at full speed for 90 seconds. Open the lid and check the tub. If it is not completely empty of water, you may have a clogged or kinked drain line.

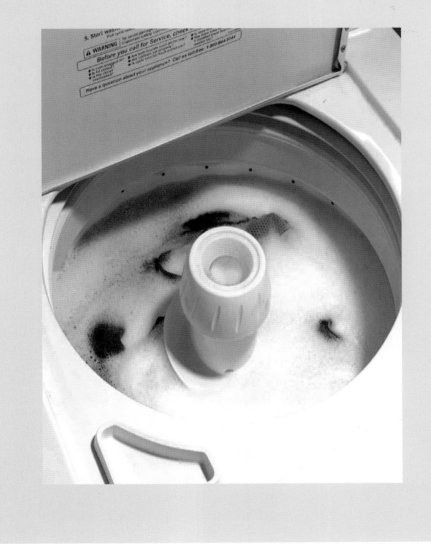

TOOLS & MATERIALS YOU NEED

❑ Channel-type pliers
❑ Small screwdriver or knife blade
❑ Old toothbrush and bowl
❑ White vinegar
❑ Stainless steel braided replacement hoses

DIFFICULTY LEVEL

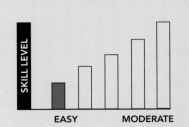

This project can be completed in a weekend.

HOW TO FIX A SLOW-FILLING WASHER

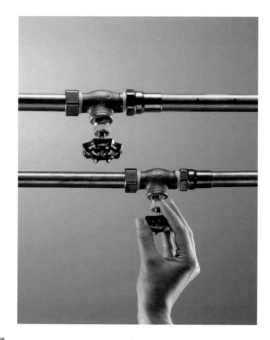

1 Start the repair by turning off the cold and hot water supply stop valves mounted in the wall, near the washer. Also make sure to unplug the power supply cord.

2 Remove the hoses from the supply faucets or hose bibs where they are connected. If you cannot turn them by hand, use channel-type pliers to turn the fittings counterclockwise to loosen them.

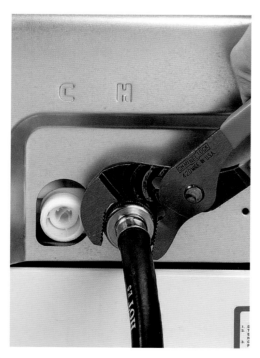

3 Remove the hoses from the back of the washing machine. Hold a bucket or bowl under each hose as it is removed to catch any water left in the line.

4 Some water supply hoses for washing machines contain filter screens in the hose couplings. If your hose couplings contain screens, remove them carefully and clean them by soaking in a vinegar solution and scrubbing with an old toothbrush. Replace the screen in the couplings.

5 If your washing machine has cone filters in the water inlet ports, remove them with a pair of needlenose pliers and inspect them for clogs.

TIP: Use an old toothbrush or any small, soft-bristled brush to clean out the cone filters. If the sediment or scaling is stubborn, soak the part in a solution of white vinegar and water. If the cone filter is in poor condition, replace it.

6 Wrap Teflon tape around the inlet ports and then twist the new hoses onto the inlet ports and the water supply valves. Hand-tighten the fittings, then snug them up with channel-type pliers. Plug in the power, turn on the water, and check for proper operation.

OTHER REASONS FOR SLOW FILLING:

• **LOW WATER PRESSURE.** Some electronic control models will time out if the washer takes longer than 20 to 40 minutes to fill. This is very difficult to fix as well as being expensive and requiring special tools.

• **PUMP FROZEN.** If the washer was stored where the temperatue is below freezing, water in the pump can freeze and lock the motor. Allow time to thaw and it should start.

• **TIMER NOT PULLED OUT COMPLETELY.** On mechanical models, be sure the timer knob is pulled out completely and set to the beginning of the cycle. It may be necessary to advance the timer slightly and pull the knob out again in case the start of the cycle varies slightly from the graphic on the control panel.

Appliance Troubleshooting Guide

GENERAL PROBLEMS WITH MAJOR APPLIANCES

No Power

Appliance is not plugged in properly.	**Solution:** Test plug to make sure it is fully seated in receptacle.
Circuit breaker or fuse controlling the appliance is tripped, or in the closed position.	**Solution:** Try to reactivate it as follows: For a circuit breaker, push the breaker to the OFF position first, then all the way back to ON. For a plug fuse, inspect the window in the fuse to see if the small metal strip inside has been broken or the glass has been scorched. Replace the fuse as needed.
Bad receptacle. Another possible reason the appliance is not receiving power is that the receptacle has failed.	**Solution:** Use a voltage probe to test the receptacle. If you've determined that a receptacle is not working, shut off power to the circuit at the service panel and then remove the coverplate. Inspect the wire connections to make sure they are sound. If they are, replace the receptacle.

WASHING MACHINE

Washing Machine Leaking or Overflowing

Water is splashing down from the overflow tube.	**Solution:** This is usually caused by oversudsing. To correct, reduce the amount of detergent that you are using. Occasionally run a wash cycle with no detergent to reduce soap build-up.
Drain hose not in drainpipe.	**Solution:** The leak will usually come out of the back of the machine. Make sure the drain hose is secured and fully inserted into the washer drain hose port prior to assembly of plastic drain.
Loose fill hose connections.	**Solution:** Test connections and tighten by hand or with channel-type pliers.
Water leaking from pump.	**Solution:** If your pump leaks, the seal has probably failed and you should have a service person replace the pump.

Washing Machine Doesn't Work

Washer lid raised.	**Solution:** Close the lid. Washing machines will not operate if the lid is not shut completely.
Lid switch probe failed. This is a small plastic piece which fits into a hole on the under side of the open lid.	**Solution:** Replace the lid switch probe.

Washing machine fills slowly

Water supply is not fully open at valve	**Solution:** Open valve.
Water valve has failed.	**Solution:** Shut off supply at nearest stop valve and replace the supply valve.
Water pressure is too low.	**Solution:** Have a plumber check supply lines for corrosion and replace as necessary. If you have a private well, inspect the pump and replace with a higher capacity model if needed.
Plugged filter screen.	**Solution:** Unplug the washer from the wall outlet and turn off the water. Pull the washer away from the wall and unscrew the hose connections. Remove the filters from the hose connectors. Clean as needed with an old toothbrush and white vinegar, or replace the screens.

DISHWASHER

Dishwasher Doesn't Run

Door not latched correctly.	**Solution:** Open the door and re-close it firmly.
Wall switch that controls dishwasher not in ON position.	**Solution:** Locate wall switch and flip switch to ON.

DISHWASHER (continued)

Does Not Wash or Rinse Well

Inadequate wash action.	**Solution:** Check the wash cycle selection. Select the appropriate cycle for the dish load. Selecting a short or light wash cycle may save water and energy, but may not provide proper wash action for a heavily soiled load. If food remains on the dishware after the cycle, a longer cycle may be required.
Water temperature too low. Water needs to be hot enough to dissolve and activate the detergent so that it works. The hot water heater should be at least 120° F.	**Solution:** If your dishwasher doesn't have an on-board heating element, it relies solely on the temperature of the incoming water to be effective. To check water temperature, run the hot water at the kitchen sink and measure the temperature of the running water with a candy or meat thermometer. Increase the output temperature of the water heater if it is less than 120°. If your dishwasher has an onboard heater, increase the temperature setting.
Wrong detergent.	**Solution.** Read your owner's manual and use only the detergents recommended by the manufacturer.

CLOTHES DRYER

Clothes Take Too Long To Dry

The damper cap (vent cover) where the vent pipe exits the wall may not be operating properly.	**Solution:** Make sure the damper cap is working by operating it with your hand to see that it moves freely.
Flexible ducting is used, and it is kinked or not installed properly.	**Solution:** Replace the vent pipe. Neither plastic nor flexible metal venting is endorsed for use in a dryer vent because of the fire hazards the material can create.
Blockage in venting.	**Solution:** A blockage can sometimes be cleared by blowing air through it with a leaf blower. Another method is to tie a rag around the end of a plumber's snake and feed that through the vent after disconnecting it from the back of the dryer to push the blockage out.
Vent ducts are too long (usually a problem only with roof vents).	**Solution:** Re-route the venting to an exterior wall closer to the dryer.
Lint filter clogged.	**Solution:** Remove and clean the lint trap (do this each time the dryer is used).
Heat control not properly set.	**Solution:** Select a different dryer setting. Check clothes labels first for washing and drying instructions.
Washer set on "gentle" cycle. On most washers, the gentle cycle (or comparable) is really just a half-speed spin cycle. The slower speed removes less water in the spin and thereby increases drying time considerably.	**Solution:** Only use the gentle wash cycle for delicates.
Dryer is overloaded. To dry properly, articles in the dryer need as much surface area as possible exposed to the heat.	**Solution:** Remove some items and never combine washer loads in one drying batch.

Dryer Runs, But Doesn't Heat

Timer selection, fabric setting, or temperature selections are incorrect.	**Solution:** The timer should be set to "Dry" and not "Fluff" or "Cool down."
Front of dryer blocked by items being dried, blocking the airflow needed to dry.	**Solution:** Redistribute clothes properly.
Gas supply is shut off.	**Solution:** Open gas shutoff valve. If you smell gas in the air, shut supply valve off and contact your gas company.

Drum Doesn't Turn

A heavy load, such as towels or blue jeans, has caused the drive belt to slip.	**Solution:** Remove some of the clothing and try again. Also see "Replacing a Dryer Drive Belt," pages 130 to 131.
Load unbalanced.	**Solution:** Remove clothes, untangle if necessary, and reload the dryer.

Dryer Stops During the Drying Cycle

The front of the dryer is blocked, which causes it to overheat and stop.	**Solution:** Reload.
Dryer is on an automatic cycle.	**Solution:** Wait. On some automatic cycles the timer will advance sporadically, so it may at times appear that it is not advancing at all.
Dryer tilted to the rear.	**Solution:** Level the dryer front to back by adjusting height of feet.

RANGES

Oven and Burners Don't Work

Gas not turned on or the electricity supply is off.	**Solution:** Turn on the gas or electrical flow as needed.

Oven Works Poorly But Burners Work Fine

Oven settings incorrect.	**Solution:** Check owner's manual and adjust settings as suggested.
Control knobs for oven temperature and oven functions not calibrated correctly (this happens often when the knobs are removed for cleaning and replaced).	**Solution:** Use oven thermometer to recalibrate knob settings.
Cracked bake or broil element (electric).	**Solution:** To identify, turn the oven on and make sure that the bake element (the one in the bottom of the oven) glows in the bake cycle. Then set the oven control to broil and watch the broil element to see if it glows. Remove and replace the bake or broil element if needed (see sidebar).

Electric Burner Doesn't Work

Electric burner or socket has failed.	**Solution:** Disconnect power. To remove the burner, lift its front edge and pull it toward yourself until it is out. To test the burner, remove a burner that does work and install the questionable burner in the good burner socket. If the burner lights up you know the receptacle is bad. If it is, replace it with one that is good. If the burner doesn't light up, the burner is the problem. Purchase a replacement and install.

Gas Burner Doesn't Work

Bad igniter. When gas flow is good but the burner won't light, the problem almost always is with the igniter (the electronic sparking device clicks when you turn the control knob to light).	**Solution:** Replace the igniter.
Pilot light is out (older models only). Failure of a pilot light to light or stay lit is usually caused by a clogged pilot hole.	**Solution:** To clean hole and relight the pilot, first turn off all the range controls, shut off gas supply and remove the burner grates. Lift the front edge of the cooktop and prop it up. Use a needle to probe and clean the pilot hole. Turn gas supply on and light a match near the pilot opening. Find the pilot adjustment screw, usually located on the side of the pilot light near the manifold at the front of the range. Adjust the flame, which should be a blue cone with sharp edges and 1/4" to 3/8" high.

HOW TO REPLACE AN OVEN ELEMENT

To remove a bake or broil element, unscrew the nuts or screws that secure the element to the back of the oven. If it's a self-cleaning element, you will find a capillary tube containing a caustic element. Wearing rubber gloves to protect your hands, unclip the capillary tube carefully and set it aside. Unscrew any supporting brackets and then pull the element toward yourself to expose the wiring. Wrap masking tape around each of the wires so you know their positions. Remove the element by unplugging it from the element terminals. Obtain replacement element from your local appliance parts store and replace by reversing the removal procedure.

GARBAGE DISPOSER

Runs But Doesn't Grind

Blades broken. If you can hear the disposer running but not accomplishing anything, the blades may be broken.

Solution: Inspect with a flashlight. If blades are broken, replace the unit.

Hums or Buzzes But Doesn't Grind

Something is stuck between the drain hole and impellers and the motor has shut off to protect it from burning out.

Solution: Remove the obstruction. First, unplug the machine from its power source (don't just turn off the wall switch). Then, use a flashlight to locate the jam. If you can't remove it with tongs or pliers, look on the bottom of the appliance for a small hex-shaped hole and a matching allen wrench. Insert the wrench in the hole and turn it back and forth to move the impellers and dislodge the material.

Water Doesn't Drain

Sink is clogged and the water is backing up.

Solution: Unclog the drain, perhaps by plunging it or removing the trap and dislodging the clog.

REFRIGERATOR

Refrigerator Not Cool Enough

Settings too low.	**Solution:** Check temperature and adjust upward.
Dust or dirt on condenser coils.	**Solution:** Vacuum or clean with brush (see page 96).
Gasket not sealing properly.	**Solution:** Replace the refrigerator door gasket (see page 97).

Water Puddles Below Appliance

Leak in drinking water dispenser or icemaker lines.	**Solution:** Test all plumbing connections and replace fittings if necessary (see pages 95 to 97).
Clogged defrost drain tube.	**Solution:** Locate drain tube from the defrost system (usually located under the floor of the freezer compartment). Clear or replace tube.
Evaporator drip pan leaks.	**Solution:** Locate the drip pan beneath the refrigerator and inspect it for leaks or to see if it is out of position. If it has a hole, replace it or repair the hole.

Frost Accumulation

Poor door seals.	**Solution:** Replace door gaskets (see page 97).
Clogged drain tube (side by side).	**Solution:** If there is ice on the floor of a side-by-side refrigerator or upright freezer, it usually means a clogged drain tube problem. To clear the drain tube, first check under a storage drawer to locate the drain opening. Using a baking syringe, force a solution of baking soda and warm water or bleach into the opening. If the clog doesn't yield, try using a length of 1/4" plastic tubing to dislodge the blockage.

Doesn't Make Ice

Water supply line is kinked or blocked.	**Solution:** Straighten out or replace the line as needed.
Blockage at saddle valve or tap valve.	**Solution:** Replace valve (see page 68).
Ice blocking fill tube.	**Solution:** If ice has backed up and is blocking the fill tube, you should thaw the icemaker. To do this, first unplug the refrigerator and remove the loose ice and the ice bin. If the refrigerator has one, remove the metal clip that holds the fill tube down, then use a squirt of hot water on the ice using a turkey baster, catching the melting water in the ice bin or some other receptacle.

REFRIGERATOR NOISE

The refrigerator can be a loud appliance. There are many "normal" refrigeration sounds. All refrigerators can moan, groan, pop, or sizzle due to higher speed compressors and other features, which older model refrigerators did not have. In addition to the compressor, there are other operating parts to perform all the many modern functions of a refrigerator. These components will have sounds associated with them. One suggestion: place a piece of rubber-backed carpeting under the unit to absorb the noise.

RESOURCES & PHOTOGRAPHY CONTRIBUTORS

Resources

National Kitchen & Bath Association
(NKBA)
800-843-6522
www.nkba.com

Plumbing and Drainage Institute
800 Turnpike Street, Suite 300
North Andover, MA 01845
www.pdionline.org

International Association of
Plumbing and Merchanical Officials
5001 E. Philadelphia St.
Ontario, CA 91761
www.iapmo.org

Plumbing, Heating, Cooling Information Bureau
222 Merchandise Mart Plaza
Chicago, IL 60654
www.phcib.org

World Plumbing Council
64 Station Lane, Hornchurch
Essex, RM12 6NB, England
www.worldplumbing.org

International Conference of Building Officials
5360 Workman Mill Rd.
Whittier, CA 90601-2298

Hakatai Enterprises, Inc.
888-6667-2429
www.hakatai.com
Tiles courtesy of Hakatai featured
        on pages 1 (left), 4, 18, 32, 54,
        61 (lower left), 62 (top left),
        73 (top right, lower left & right).

Photography Contributors

InSinkErator
800-558-5700
www.insinkerator.com
Page 58

GE, General Electric
800-626-2005
www.geappliances.com
Pages 8, 21, 27, 33, 70, 122

CONVERSION CHARTS

Metric Equivalents

Inches (in.)	1/64	1/32	1/25	1/16	1/8	1/4	3/8	2/5	1/2	5/8	3/4	7/8	1	2	3	4	5	6	7	8	9	10	11	12	36	39.4
Feet (ft.)																								1	3	3 1/12
Yards (yd.)																									1	1 1/12
Millimeters (mm)	0.40	0.79	1	1.59	3.18	6.35	9.53	10	12.7	15.9	19.1	22.2	25.4	50.8	76.2	101.6	127	152	178	203	229	254	279	305	914	1,000
Centimeters (cm)							0.95	1	1.27	1.59	1.91	2.22	2.54	5.08	7.62	10.16	12.7	15.2	17.8	20.3	22.9	25.4	27.9	30.5	91.4	100
Meters (m)																								.30	.91	1.00

Converting Measurements

TO CONVERT:	TO:	MULTIPLY BY:
Inches	Millimeters	25.4
Inches	Centimeters	2.54
Feet	Meters	0.305
Yards	Meters	0.914
Miles	Kilometers	1.609
Square inches	Square centimeters	6.45
Square feet	Square meters	0.093
Square yards	Square meters	0.836
Cubic inches	Cubic centimeters	16.4
Cubic feet	Cubic meters	0.0283
Cubic yards	Cubic meters	0.765
Pints (U.S.)	Liters	0.473 (Imp. 0.568)
Quarts (U.S.)	Liters	0.946 (Imp. 1.136)
Gallons (U.S.)	Liters	3.785 (Imp. 4.546)
Ounces	Grams	28.4
Pounds	Kilograms	0.454
Tons	Metric tons	0.907

TO CONVERT:	TO:	MULTIPLY BY:
Millimeters	Inches	0.039
Meters	Feet	3.28
Kilometers	Miles	0.621
Square meters	Square feet	10.8
Cubic centimeters	Cubic inches	0.061
Cubic meters	Cubic yards	1.31
Liters	Quarts (U.S.)	1.057 (Imp. 0.88)
Grams	Ounces	0.035
Metric tons	Tons	1.1

Converting Temperatures

Convert degrees Fahrenheit (F) to degrees Celsius (C) by following this simple formula: Subtract 32 from the Fahrenheit temperature reading. Then, mulitply that number by 5/9. For example, 77°F - 32 = 45. 45 × 5/9 = 25°C.

To convert degrees Celsius to degrees Fahrenheit, multiply the Celsius temperature reading by 9/5. Then, add 32. For example, 25°C × 9/5 = 45. 45 + 32 = 77°F.

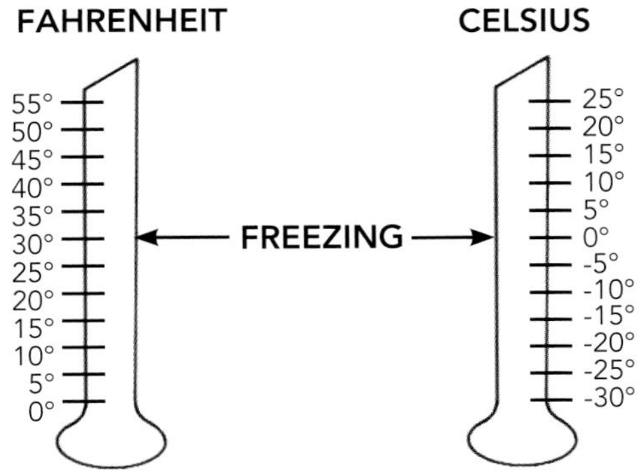

INDEX

Also From **CREATIVE PUBLISHING international**

Complete Guide to Bathrooms

Complete Guide Build Your Kids a Treehouse

Complete Guide to Ceramic & Stone Tile

Complete Guide to Creative Landscapes

Complete Guide to Decks

Complete Guide to Dream Kitchens

Complete Guide to Easy Woodworking Projects

Complete Guide to Finishing Walls & Ceilings

Complete Guide to Flooring

Complete Guide to Gazebos & Arbors

Complete Guide to Home Carpentry

Complete Guide to Home Plumbing

Complete Guide to Home Wiring

Complete Guide to Landscape Construction

Complete Guide Maintain Your Pool & Spa

Complete Guide to Masonry & Stonework

Complete Guide to Outdoor Wood Projects

Complete Guide to Painting & Decorating

Complete Guide to Patios

Complete Guide to Roofing & Siding

Complete Guide to Trim & Finish Carpentry

Complete Guide to Windows & Doors

Complete Guide to Wood Storage Projects

Complete Guide to Yard & Garden Features

Complete Outdoor Builder

Complete Photo Guide to Home Repair

Complete Photo Guide to Home Improvement

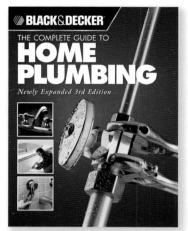

ISBN 1-58923-201-1

ISBN 1-58923-213-5

Creative Publishing international

18705 Lake Drive East • Chanhassen, MN 55317 • www.creativepub.com